ICONOGRAPH

ICONOGRAPHY
A Writer's Meditation

Susan Neville

INDIANA
University Press
Bloomington & Indianapolis

This book is a publication of

Indiana University Press
601 North Morton Street
Bloomington, IN 47404-3797 USA

http://iupress.indiana.edu

Telephone orders   800-842-6796
Fax orders   812-855-7931
Orders by e-mail   iuporder@indiana.edu

The paper used in this publication meets the minimum require-
ments of American National Standard for Information Sciences—
Permanence of Paper for Printed Library Materials, ANSI Z39.48-
1984.

Manufactured in the United States of America

Library of Congress Cataloging-in-Publication Data

Neville, Susan.
  Iconography : a writer's meditation / Susan Neville.
    p. cm.
  ISBN 0-253-34322-4 (alk. paper) — ISBN 0-253-21614-1
(pbk. : alk. paper)
    1. Neville, Susan—Authorship. 2. Icon painting.
3. Authorship. I. Title.
  PS3564.E8525Z466 2003
  813'.54—dc21
                                            2003005882

1 2 3 4 5 08 07 06 05 04 03

For
Steven,
Laura,
Allison,
and
Matthew

We shall rest and we shall see,
we shall see and we shall love,
we shall love and we shall praise,
in the end which is no end.

—St. Augustine

CONTENTS

Acknowledgments

With thanks to Mother Catherine and the members of the icon class; to everyone in Freelance Nation—Ken, Greg, Julie, Duncan, Charlie; to my friends and readers on this project—Kendra Boileau Stokes, Michael Martone, Maura Stanton, Jane Lyle; and to my colleagues at Butler University and my family—for constant inspiration.

ST. MARY OF ENNUI

The hardest thing to learn is to trust the process.
—Mother Catherine Westin

1

In Indianapolis, Indiana, when the race cars run, there's a weird semi-mystical hum in the air like that sound you get when you run your finger around the top of a water glass. Stand fifteen miles away from the track, and still you can hear the sound. It's a constant backdrop, the strange and endless blue screen of the existential hum.

October, 1999, the first Formula One race at the Speedway, the last few months of a century. Prince Andrew and Fergie had rented opposite floors of the Canterbury Hotel, and Melanie Griffith and Antonio Banderas a house in Zionsville. They'd descended from the clouds, and we could feel their immanence. At any moment we might catch a glimpse of them, their faces emerging from the crowd and catching at our throats.

It was a perfect hour for visions. Late in the day, right before sunset. The sky was as clear and blue as a cat's-eye marble, but everything else was on fire: a ribbon of yellow-orange at the horizon, the faint orange of street lights, the yellow of fire hydrants and lines painted down the center of the highway, red tail-lights on cars. And every reflective surface in the world reflecting the setting sun, and all the trees ochre, bronze, olive, cinnamon, and crimson like the cushions in the autumn Pottery Barn catalogue.

While the rest of the city was heading to the race or a restaurant, I was driving to an icon-painting class. My husband was sure I'd lost my mind. A class on Friday nights, from seven to ten. How many Fridays will it take? he asked, and I said I didn't know, maybe a month? But you're not an artist, he said, and you're not Catholic. In fact, he said, you have terrible handwriting, and you're not even a lukewarm Methodist. I know, I said. But like the sound of the cars, the sense that I should do this had gotten under my skin.

Think of it as an affair, I said, and he said that would be more understandable.

I had developed an infatuation with the words *icon, iconography, iconoclast,* and *iconographer* in the same way that a visual artist might develop an obsession with the color blue. I wanted to write with those words and needed to clothe them in something concrete. There were these other icons I could have followed on that night—the hotel-dwelling, more-familiar-to-me icons—but I chose to follow this one. In particular I loved the music of the word *iconographer*—the five-syllable mix of hard consonants and soft vowels, the way it moves in your mouth from the breath in the throat to the back of the palate, and then the tongue rocking across the mouth's roof to the "ahh" in the center (as though in appreciation of the rocking), to the back of the mouth again with that hard "g," and the finale between the lower lip and upper tooth. *Iconographer.* A high-calorie word. You could live on just the sounds.

— — —

I had put this class off for at least two years and would have continued to put it off except that two days before I'd fallen down a flight of marble stairs, and it wasn't a simple fall. It was the kind of fall where you feel your feet give out and suddenly you're flying through the air like falling from a window, and you feel your hip, your cheekbone, your thigh, the parts of your body as they hit the sharp edge of each step, your body thudding down the space like any material object—a shoe, say—and you have absolutely no control over it, and when you hit the landing you can't remember any of it. It's the kind of fall where people break their necks and become paralyzed or die. It was that hard, that unexpected.

It felt like I was thrown. There was the force of all the gravity in the universe behind the fall, and nothing I could do or say would stop it once it had begun.

Of course I had my arms full of books, and of course I was late, and of course I was in too much of a hurry, and of course I had on a long black lycra skirt that somehow caught itself around the heel of my shoe the very day I'd depended on my body's knowledge of those familiar stairs and hadn't held on to anything.

I guess I screamed. Several people came out of their offices to help me, and their faces emerged out of a fog. They were kind, angelic faces, offering me a place to sit and a cool drink, running for bags of ice from the zoology lab across campus, and asking if they could drive me home. I thanked my rescuers and sat for fifteen minutes holding the ice on my face, then thanked them again and got in the car and began to drive. I held a sweating paper cup of ice against my cheekbone to keep the swelling down, and I checked my pupils in the mirror to see if they were enlarged. I felt a lump rising on my leg and another on my arm, and the next day there were more large lumps on my belly and my hip. They turned particularly noxious shades of Baudelairean green and eggplant purple and felt, in fact, like eggplants were rising underneath the skin. And I kept seeing the stairs in my imagination, how tomb-like the marble had looked rising above me, and I kept shuddering, realizing how hard I'd been thrown.

As I sat there after the fall, a business card was the last thing my rescuers picked up from the floor and handed to me. How did it get there? It was a card I'd received from an Orthodox nun I'd met at an art fair. Greek? Russian? I wasn't sure. She'd given me her card (she had a card), and I'd somehow held on to it, though not consciously. The card had a way of appearing in coat pockets and the bottoms of purses or on the floor of my car or in my desk drawer at work, and I'd never thrown it away. I always leave art shows and antique and home shows with a pocket full of cards, always thinking I'll have that bathroom re-tiled, that I'll save to buy that landscape painting, that I'll have someone out to check for mold in the crawlspace. The cards are always in the wastebasket before the week is out.

But for some reason I'd kept her card. I guess I'd have to say she made an impression on me. She wasn't like any other artist at the fair. I'd gone through tent after tent of artists, all with business cards and their signatures scrawled across the bottoms of their paintings, and here was this woman who had sculptures and icons she'd painted hanging in cathedrals and country churches in Europe and Africa (as I found out much later), and not a one had her name on it. If a church history mentions the origin of the icon, it would say the name of the monastery and the city. Even her business card had the name St. Andrew Rublev School of Iconography and not her name.

Mother Catherine, she was called, or the Nun Catherine. She wore a simple brown cotton habit, like a monk's habit but with a nun's hat, whatever they're called, no collar. Nothing like a television nun, she was slender and young—mid to late thirties—with milk-chocolate skin and Buddy Holly glasses with black plastic frames. When I met her, she was standing in front of a triptych covered with her students' icons, not hers, and the icons were oddly beautiful and stylized and glowed with that deep-down iconographic light. There was something about the care with which they were painted, about the images themselves and particularly about that light, that made the tents of nostalgic Midwestern photographs and pottery seem lovely but ephemeral. The whole exhibit seemed so out of place somehow, so, well, Byzantine. But it felt real. There was nothing ironic about it, and you couldn't respond to it ironically—unlike the other unironic art, the paintings of barns and foliage. My response to the art felt oddly pure. I had no words or theories or beliefs to come between me and my experience of it.

I said I was interested in the class, and she gave me a schedule for the school. I told her I couldn't paint, that I had never been able to paint. She said it didn't matter, that the process was something you learned to trust, and that the medium itself was very forgiving.

I started to say that I wasn't religious, but I didn't, and she didn't ask. I'm not Catholic—not even a Protestant—not Jewish, not a Buddhist or a follower of Islam, not New Age, not Wiccan, not nationalistic, not a Jungian, not a Satanist, not an art critic, not a consumer of health foods. Have I left anything out? I'm not a Sufi. I'm not a Scientologist, and I'm definitely not orthodox in any sense. But I did know that I wanted to paint an icon, and I said it was because I loved the word. She couldn't hear, I thought, the lower-case "w."

2

The monastery was an old wood-framed house with blue paint peeling off the sides in long strips, like carrot curls. The crime rate in that section of the city was, I knew, five times the national average. A block beyond was where the male prostitutes walked the street, and even the Joy of All Who Sorrow Church around the corner had gated windows.

There were eight people gathered on the front porch of the house. The women looked like moths, fragile and lovely. There were two men. For one second in the apricot-colored sunset, chain link across the street, a drug deal going on in the shadows of the vacant weed-filled lots, the nun in costume like a scene from some oil painting, I had one momentary flash of Halloween—that windy apple-scented thrill, that feeling. The sun shifted then to gray. We were halfway through the year from Easter. I wanted a different life, the one that would start the new year in December. I wanted to break through into the new millennium as someone who belonged to something. Why look here? Drug deals in the shadows, men cruising the street for sex, and pilgrims waiting for me to join them on the dilapidated porch. Just ahead of me I could see the glass and steel of the city, could feel the hum of race cars, the excitement of princesses and rock stars in guest suites a mile away. We were the only ones aware this night that in the middle of it all stood this anachronistic house with a hand-lettered sign announcing that it was a monastic community. I felt odd getting out of my car to join them. Why are you here? they might ask, and I would have to say I really didn't know. To say that I'm a writer didn't seem like the complete answer. Anything I might say would feel like a partial truth and a partial lie. Beside the door there was a small icon in a box, and a sign: *St. Andrew Rublev School of Iconography.*

I stepped across the threshold, and into the gloom. I would spend the next few months learning how an icon is made: In layers of light. Of mineral and wood. Of yolk and blood, and earth and time.

3

Where's the gold leaf? The tracing paper? Has anyone seen the compass? It's under papers somewhere. Could you pull the carpet squares away from the corner of the cement floor where the ground damp is seeping in, Mother Catherine asks, and did anyone leave the hot plate on? I smell hot glue.

And the light bulbs keep going dim, I think, and there are no screens in the upstairs windows. All around, the house is decaying, and we're focused on single rectangles of oak and ash.

This is the workshop in the cellar of the monastery. Tables covered with oilcloth, ancient appliances—the hot plate, a slide projector, thirty-year-old fans with thick, fraying cords. There's a square metal sink in the cellar, one of those sinks made for doing hand washing in the early part of the last century, one step up from beating your clothing with a stone on a riverbank. The sink is filled with plastic paint palettes and baby food jars and a vague smell of rotting egg. A household of Marys without a Martha. I find out quickly that if you have a question about art history or science, you'll get it answered. In this class alone, there's an entire library of information stored in our collective brain cells. You want to discuss Paul Tillich or medieval architecture, this is your place. But it will take you a while to find a thing that you've misplaced—the brush, the cup, the blade, the sketch. (As it turns out, over the weeks, this seems to be my one and only skill. As in my own home, I'm the Finder of Lost Things.)

The first week we choose our board. The board supports the icon, we're told, and the choice of board is in itself important. It has to be non-resinous: linden, oak, ash, or beech. The boards have been drying for months, waiting for us.

We sand our board, two hours of sanding and leveling. I had

expected to jump right in with color, to get this thing done within a class or two. I had told my husband I'd be gone for three Fridays at the most. That's the way things are usually done. Who would expect otherwise? I had expected my icon to look like a cartoon of an icon since I couldn't paint, but I expected to learn something by watching the real pilgrims. What I didn't expect to do was spend hours in a basement sanding or to find out that it could take up to a year to finish it, and I didn't know at the time that it would take me even longer.

Toward the end of the first class, we made our first pan of rabbit-hide glue—the crystal substance mixed with water and heated. We painted it on our board and covered the board with cheesecloth and then cut the excess cheesecloth from the edge. I went home that first night with my board and a baggie of the crystals and a brush and instructions for cooking up pots of glue in my own kitchen. For the next week, at prescribed intervals, I would paint the wood and cheesecloth with the invisible paint. I'm an infamously bad cook, as was my grandmother, who would begin to boil an egg and get sidetracked by a book or sewing, and the next thing she knew, the egg would explode in the pan and end up on the ceiling. But I had to stay with this, to concentrate my attention on the mixture. Glue that is overcooked will lose its strength. Glue that is insufficiently boiled can cause cracks, later, in the image. How much later? Somewhere in some distant century.

The next week, Mother Catherine promised, we would begin the gesso.

You can buy gesso ready-made in any art store, and you can paint an icon quickly with acrylics, but that's a process from this time, and the process we've undertaken is the medieval one. Buying an acrylic gesso is like planting a silver maple rather than a beech tree. You'll see the silver maple grow before your eyes; it will shade you in your lifetime if it isn't blown down in some summer storm. A beech tree is more sturdy but will take generations to grow into maturity.

We cook the gesso on a hot plate. It's made of the same rabbit-hide glue and chalk, and we cook and cook it until it's ready to be painted on the boards. The gesso is pure white and thick and messy, and we have to wait patiently between coats for it to dry, and then we sand it, over and over for weeks, until the surface is as hard as porcelain.

Now and then someone will leave a bubble on the surface, and only Mother Catherine will see it. A bubble, she says, can rise up through the layers centuries later and make a pockmark on the skin. That's why you pray, that's why you pay attention, that's why we use so many different grades of sandpaper and we look at each board with so many eyes.

Did I mention that we pray? Or rather, that we sing and pray, depending on the reason each of us has for being here. At the beginning of each class Mother Catherine lights an altar candle, and we sing in front of a mantle of gorgeous icons, and those of us who are Catholic or Episcopalian or Orthodox venerate the icons, and those of us who are Protestant or artists simply sing.

For some reason I feel so holy sitting in this basement working on a portrait of the Virgin Mary. Perhaps these hours will in themselves wash away my many many sins.

When the gessoing is done, we take sharp blades and etch copies of the original image onto our own small square of board. We did a graphite transfer first, covering a sheet of paper with pencil lead and then laying the graphite over the board and tracing the image prototype. It is this image that we now etch onto the board. If your hand cuts too sharp, Mother Catherine says, you have to start again from the beginning. You have to cut into the gesso deep enough so that you can see the image when you hold it the right way in the light, but not deep enough to touch the wood. It has to be something you can *sense* is there but not necessarily *see,* like a scratch on your own skin.

If you take your eyes away from the prototype, Mother Catherine says, if you insert your own ego in any way, you'll make mistakes.

The image, she says, is always the reflection of the prototype. What is intelligible and touches the conscious mind is only the exterior surface of the icon. Its essence is to be a point of contact, a place where we meet with a presence, with mystery. The icon is a window into the invisible.

I learn to dry an egg yolk on the skin of my hand. I cup the yolk between my index and middle fingers, pinch the membrane, and let the inside of the yolk fall into the jar. You throw the skin away. You've used the dryness of your own skin to make the membrane stick to you. You add vinegar and some water so that the mass of the yolk is doubled. How much water exactly? someone asks, and Mother Catherine says she's never measured an egg yolk. You just have to pay attention.

The egg wash is applied to the board each time we begin to paint. It's kept in a baby food jar until it begins to smell or until the bottom hardens into sediment.

Before we begin to apply the colors, the gessoed boards are blessed. IESOUS CHRISTOS NIKA (Jesus Christ Conquers), Mother Catherine says, and "all diverse powers are shattered in the name of the Father and of the Son and of the Holy Spirit amen." Mother Catherine paints a slash of red along the outside edge to keep the demons out, to bless the space like the blood on the door at Passover.

She tells us about students whose sins have appeared on the board, about the colors turning into mud. I'm sure that this will happen to me. Even at the end, she says, you have to pray and bless the oil before you pour it on the finished icon. The whole thing, all those months and months of work, could bleed away.

There's a woman in the class who's a professional violinist. Her name is Sally. At one time she majored in math and science. Now she plays her violin in bluegrass bands, and she works in this funky violin shop where I rented my son's string bass when he was in junior high school orchestra. It was a huge metal bass with wood-colored paint, a bass that troop musicians carried during the Second World War. There were indentations all over the surface, and my son was sure that they were bullet holes.

Mother Catherine says that I have sanded well, that my board is well-tempered. Well-tempered means in tune with itself, Sally tells me, and it seems to have something to do with discrete mathematical functions which she describes and which I'll never understand. In tempered tuning everyone's in tune with a keyboard and it sounds off-key, she says. It's a square-root function rather than a whole-number function. I see, I say, but of course I don't.

The paint is made with tints found in clay and plants and blood. An ochre for Mary's face, a rusty red for the robe, gold leaf for the halo. The paint is applied in multiple layers, from dark to light, and every act and every brush stroke is symbolic. It's an exacting process, but if you make a mistake, it's the egg tempera that allows you to confess to your teacher and erase the mistake rather than, as with acrylic, simply covering it over.

You can repair any mistake you make or have made, she says, by going clear down through the layers of the previous week's work, down through the lighter paint to the darker, down through the gold leaf, down through the layers of animal and mineral. The farther you go with your erasing brush, the darker the image gets, until you're down to the pure solid light again of glaze.

Sometimes the work is dangerous. The X-acto blade can slip when you're cutting the lines in the gesso, and many of the paints are poisonous. Mother Catherine talks about an artist whose cat got into the cadmium and her fur turned pink. Cadmium bonds to the bones, she says, like calcium, and it can turn your teeth and nails as pink as if you'd washed them with a red sweatshirt. It's a noxious poison, like lead.

Other colors are relatively harmless. Titanium is in your toothpaste, it's in your pills. When mixing colors, you use it sparingly. The tiniest bit can wash a color out.

Ultramarine red. Cerulean blue and vergone green for the virgin's underscarf. 4870 red looks like dried blood, and I wonder if it is. It would have been, Mother Catherine says, in the old days. But this is just iron oxide. It hasn't been near any dead people.

Cobalt means to mine spirit, a classmate tells me. She goes into a long story about the history of cobalt mines.

If you hard-boil eggs in onion skins, they turn sepia, I'm told.

The tears of Mary are yellow, orange, and red.

4

I spent one afternoon painting the "shower cap" around the virgin's face, the thin line of aqua on a deeper blue. Three hours I concentrated on this eighth-of-an-inch rendering of cloth.

Nothing will be more difficult or time-consuming, I'm told, than those layers of highlights on the face. Eight different layers of paint from a sunburned red to ochre, a week of drying after each layer to achieve the proper luminosity.

It's hot in here, we say. Mother Catherine says that each human being gives off six hundred watts.

A light goes out overhead, and she stands on a ladder to replace the bulb. Only sixty watts, less than a human being. She washes dead spiders out of the globe.

The evening I spent painting the aqua around the bonnet, I left in the dark, and when I looked up, I saw the same line of aqua in the neon strip around the bank tower.

This starts to happen every week. Whatever stroke I spend the three hours working on becomes, for several hours, the lens I look through.

The monastic life is supposed to be like the flower of a culture, Mother Catherine says one night, but at this particular time it's not connected. Like the feathering, I say, the highlights on the face. (Where you tilt the board and dab a more intense version of the color you've just used so the intensity pools and then shades gradually into the earlier highlights. Only now the board's not tipped. It starts watered down and pools and gathers at the bone. It makes a difference.)

Much of every class is spent literally watching paint dry. You have to wait after each color, each layer. So many colors. You learn to see them, and then to see through them. Meudon white, white lead, white silver, zinc white, titanium, Naples yellow, cadmium, Indian yellow, chromium, yellow ochre, red ochre, Mars yellow, English red, Pompeii red, sienna, burnt sienna, umber, Chinese vermilion, cadmium, alizarin lacquer, Helios red, ultramarine, cobalt, cerulean blue, Prussian blue, Berlin blue, Paris blue, chromium green, emerald, cobalt green, green earth Veronese, true dark cobalt violet, vine black, ivory black, bone black (obtained by burning bones).

Sometimes while I'm waiting for my last stroke of paint to dry, I read. I'll bring my own book or read the ones lining the wall above Mother Catherine's desk. Sometimes I'll just sit quietly and look at the icons in the room. I like to watch the Seeker of the Lost. The virgin's fingers are light string beans. Christ's left hand angles down around his mother's cheek; his right hand is fat and flat with those thin fingers, like a chocolate turtle. His torso is long, his legs short, but where the face of Christ touches the face of his mother, there's incandescence. The Seeker of the Lost is the only virgin with hair. There are sparkling jewels along her robe. The jewels are stars. Stare long enough and you fall right through them. The universe crystallized in just this way, you fall through them into another universe and on and on and on into the extraordinary beauty of complexity.

An icon is an open door and not a whitewashed wall.

5

Suddenly, for some reason, my hand doesn't want to learn the brush strokes. If I don't think too much about what I'm doing, I can do it, but I always think too much. And I get impatient. In some places you want the paint to be opaque, and you simply saturate the brush and let the colors pool on the wood. The etched line holds in the edge; the molecules stick together like water on the top of a glass. At other times you want translucency, a thinner coat. You dip the brush, wipe off the excess, flatten it out almost like a string mop. If you load the brush and then paint until it's empty, you'll get a wave effect. For a while my effects were right, and then for whatever reason my effects were always wrong.

It was even worse the night we put the gold leaf on the halo. Gold sticks to whatever is moist or sticky. The gold we use is Patten gold, stuck to the paper with static electricity. As you're applying the size, you hold the icon in your hand and use the light to make sure you haven't missed a spot. If you've missed a spot, don't go back and get it, Mother Catherine says. If you go back in without experience, she says, it will make the lump uneven. She will make our corrections for us. When we're done, we'll wait until the gold size on the halo is dry and then rub a wet finger on the size to remove any lint. The night we apply the gold, we know not to wear anything with fiber that might float into the air, like a sweater.

I lay the gold on the size and rub. The gold should come right off the paper and stick to the board. Instead, the gold sticks to my fingers, to the table, to the paper, to anything but the place where the halo should be shining.

I've made so many vows before, and I've broken them as

though they were nothing.⌋ I feel like giving up. I'll never finish this.

I look around at my classmates, who all seem to be doing well. A woman named Marussa sits beside me at the table. Her hair is short, like a nun's hair, and she hardly ever talks. She only asks questions. Her icon is perfect, and I tell her so.

Oh no, she says. The iconographer from the Russian monastery is flying into Canada this summer, and I have a lot of work to do before then.

Work? I ask.

He was such a holy man, she said, to be around him, I have to get ready.

I can't imagine it, what she's talking about. She grew up in the Orthodox church. She's worked for months on this icon, and it's beautiful. She sings all the prayers in Russian.

I swept the floor for him for two years, she says, and I asked and asked if I could make paint, and he said be patient, that if I were patient I might be ready in twenty years to paint my own, and here I am, and I'm still not sure I'm ready.

I've been sitting beside her for two months, getting it all wrong, I think.

I felt I didn't belong there, next to Marussa. My icon was going to be the one with a demonic stare, the one that disappears when Mother Catherine drops the oil. It's what I deserve.

The boy with blond hair and metal rings like halos on his ears places a thin cellphone by his painting of the mother of God. He's hard of hearing, he says, and his real mother may need to call him. He bows deeply when he comes into the room. I can't imagine what goes on inside his head. He was supposed to miss tonight's class, but here he is; he couldn't stay away.

It's hot, a woman says, and she opens the inner window. There's a grid of iron facing out onto the city sidewalk. Soon the outside world turns dark as a plum, the grate across the window shaped not like bars but like a flower.

We turn off the magnifying lamps to cool the air. *Pray that I get this right.* The boy's hand is shaking. *Pray that I get this right.* Marussa, the former nun, touches her shoulder from the right to left; she holds out her right hand and folds two fingers in toward her palm. The Father and the Son, she says, the Holy Spirit, and she crosses herself.

The iconographer from Russia never slept in a bed from the day that he became a monk, she says. Where did he sleep? I ask. He never slept, she says. You could talk to him, of course, and he'd be sitting up and you'd hear him snore, but he could talk to you and remember what you said; he never really was fully asleep.

And he's coming now across the ocean, he's heading this way, and I'll get to see him, and he told me I might be ready in twenty years, and now it's been twenty years and here I am.

She had asked Mother Catherine to bless her icon in Russian. This is why your halo shines like chrome, I said. No one else's halo shines like that.

— — —

Who am I to walk in off the street and think that I could do this? Why are you here? Marussa asks. Because of grief, I say. I didn't know I was going to say that. For what? Marussa asks. I'm not exactly sure, I say, but it feels like grief. Time passing. Love. I don't know. Perhaps something's headed this way, I say, across some ocean, and I need to be prepared for it.

Twenty years and she's got it absolutely right. Like chrome, her halo shines, smooth and odd and perfect like the inside of a bicycle wheel that's turning at high speed in some brilliant sunlight, a gold-leaf halo glistening on the gessoed boards like a wedding ring spinning across the table.

6

I knew right then that I wouldn't be coming back. I wasn't ready for this, and I thought that I might never be. The incomplete face of my icon would lie there forever on the gesso, the eyes pupilless and rimmed. I would never, I thought then, finish it.

I painted the dark background but left before I reached the light. My Virgin Mary was a murky weed-choked green, like something submerged several inches beneath the surface of an inland lake. She looked heroin-addicted, and she would rest on her dusty cellar shelf alongside other heroin-addicted Marys, waiting to be pulled up to the surface of the water and out into the air where she could be seen, an idea cloaked in flesh or paint, an image.

There are rows of unfinished Marys in the cellar. Marys of the middle-aged and of the elderly, Marys of the guilty and of the grieving. Marys of the curious and Marys of the psychotic and Marys of the suicidal and of the restless and Marys of the artist and of the non-artist and Marys of the devout and of the faithless, of the incarcerated and of the supposed free.

I wasn't ready, I told Mother Catherine when she called a few weeks later to ask why I hadn't been to class. I felt wrong doing it, I said. I felt I was there under false pretenses, I said. So prepare yourself, she said, and I said how? Tomorrow is the first day of Lent, she said. Make a vow, she said, and try to keep it.

BOOK ONE: TRANSFIGURATION

What is the meaning of life? That was all—a simple question; one that tended to close in on one with years. The great revelation had never come. The great revelation perhaps never did come. Instead there were little daily miracles, illuminations, matches struck unexpectedly in the dark. . . .

—Virginia Woolf, *To the Lighthouse*

Ash Wednesday, 2000

The first Ash Wednesday of the new millennium, and I went to the mall to buy a pair of socks. I thought about going to church but didn't. Why start now? I've never in my life been to church on Ash Wednesday. All week long I'd noticed Ash Wednesday signs along the highway and thought that if my vow was to write every day during Lent, then I should somehow begin it in a church.

But which church would I go to? I had no idea. Maybe one with jazz, where the preacher spoke poetry and there were bagels for dessert. They advertise these things in the Saturday paper. There's one that takes place in a dinner theater.

When the day arrived, I canceled a dinner engagement, saying I had something else to do. The something else was to celebrate Ash Wednesday.

But of course I ended up at the mall, where everyone looked exactly like me. We were women who'd run from our houses looking for something, and I have to admit I did feel somewhat better. The wall colors in Restoration Hardware lifted my spirits. There was a new tangerine scent in Bath and Body Works. Liz Claiborne had brought out some nice tomato-colored sweaters, and at the Bobbi Brown counter in Jacobson's I saw one of the women news anchors trying on lipstick. She was taller than I'd imagined, and she was wearing red. She was a goddess. I didn't know you'd remarried, the makeup artist was saying to her, and I almost called out to him. *Are you kidding?* She married Clyde, her co-anchor, and it was a thrilling scandal. It livened up our winter. For years on the evening news he'd shown us pictures of his wife and kids while he sat there, night after night, having the six-o-clock-how-was-your-day-honey evening chat with Diane. It was inevitable. I'm so happy now that we're married, Diane said to the makeup artist.

I couldn't wait to tell someone I'd seen her, heard her whisper her beloved's name over the wax and fragrance.

I walked from one end of the mall to the other. Everyone was white and middle-class. Everyone was a woman. Everyone's hair had highlights. Everyone was wearing black. I was wearing black. I'd had my photograph taken that morning for a book dust jacket. I knew that black was slimming. I always wear black. Why are you in mourning? my husband had asked, and I said I didn't think I was. I'd had my picture taken in an old factory. There was a Stutz Bearcat under a tarp in the background, metal ribbons hanging loose from the ceiling, spools of cable on the ground and iron pulleys. When I put my purse down on the ground and picked it up, it was covered with white dust. I got dust on my dress and black grease on my hands when I leaned against a door for the photo.

When I left the mall at closing time, there was a woman saying she'd been too tired to buy a thing. She hardly ever went to the mall without buying something, even if it was just a bar of soap. We commiserated. We'd walked through the mall like sleepwalkers. How many days of our lives had we spent in the chill of a department store? I'd hate to add it up.

Ash Wednesday. Ink stains and dust on my hands and nylon purse. Eyeliner pencil marks where I'd tried them on my hand. Everywhere I'd gone, all day long, I'd covered myself with ashes. There was no good way around it.

Buying Time

I woke up Thursday morning feeling like I had a hangover. Is there a name for the second day of Lent?

I'm not a religious person. Yesterday my neighbor decided to post the Ten Commandments in his yard, and for some reason I wanted to shoot him. I'm the pathetic character in a Flannery O'Connor story.

How many sins have I committed in just this one morning? Most of them, I'd say. There was wrath, which I've already mentioned. And sloth. I didn't take a shower until ten, and I didn't exercise, though I wanted to, and I didn't start writing this until late in the afternoon, and the only reason I did was because if I didn't, I thought I'd slit my wrists.

What did I do with this day? If you must know, I bought some perfume. The woman who sold it to me said she wanted to be my fragrance lady. I bought the national fragrance of Norway, and right now, as I'm typing this on Friday, I can smell it on my arms. Mea culpa.

Think mountains and clear skies and a little bit of ocean, my fragrance lady said. Her talent, obviously, is tying scenery to fragrances. She had a European accent, the kind of accent you could never imagine saying *think Indianapolis in the middle of the gray season, think a downtown retail cathedral, think underground parking garage, think women on day trips from New Castle and Elwood, think escalators and acres of glittering merchandise, think this place, today, right now, even if it hurts.*

Her voice was hypnotic, and she had an accent. So I thought Norway. I thought mountains and oceans and blond hair, as she'd suggested. This fragrance would, I was convinced of it, change my very life. So I bought it.

My sins. I bought the larger size and wanted to buy another brand just in case Norway didn't come through for me and lift my funk. And then later my slothful, wrathful, greedy self got angry at an office email (which I accessed from home to feel as though I'd done something productive), and I felt vain and envious when I saw the Ash Wednesday pictures of myself, which brought me face to face as well with gluttony. I'm saving lust and pride for later in this process.

Did I mention self-absorption?

If you saw my picture, or you knew me, you'd think I was sweet.

The second day of Lent I did in fact give up wine for one night. I needed to do something. And I cooked an actual meal with vegetables and several sources of calcium for my family, and I tried to be less cranky. And in the afternoon I went to the bookstore and stood in front of the religion section, looking for something good by Paul Tillich. He's always made me feel better about myself. There is faith, he says, in every serious doubt. I'm such a doubter that of course I doubt even that.

Tillich's ashes are buried in New Harmony, Indiana, down in the pocket of the state. Tillich had a long-standing affair with one of his married students, and he had, it's said, a large collection of religious pornography. Shame and guilt and duplicity can be extraordinary fuels.

Religion is right by the self-help and hypochondriac medical books, so all of us in that aisle felt somewhat embarrassed. I thought that buying a book might make me feel better about the perfume and the socks, so I looked up Ash Wednesday in an encyclopedia of Christianity to see what I should have done. I learned that Lent has something to do with Christ's forty days in the wilderness, but the whole thing lasts forty-six days because of Sundays, which disappear into some spiritual wormhole. The encyclopedia was right next to Augustine's *Confessions,* which I'd never read. I decided to read them. Why not? Maybe he has even more to confess than I do. The woman standing next to me was looking up symptoms in the Merck. We all wanted to know if we were dying, and the outlook wasn't good. I went to sleep that night on half a sleeping pill but woke up at three A.M. in a cold sweat.

A Vow

The third day of Lent, and I've had too much coffee. I want to further confess my sins, but I've hidden them too long, even from myself. I know that everyone's most secret sins have to do with love. How can you trust me? I have many good qualities, I'm sure, but often, lately, it feels as though there's nothing solid at the core.

I've never given anything up for Lent; why should I? But this year I will keep a vow. For these forty-some days I'll keep a record of my life. I want to see if there's a shape to it. I want to see if I can be changed by something. I'm not interested in a conversion experience, just something sweet and slow and tranquilizing.

So what if you start a process like this and you end up in the same place where you began? I think that people usually start these things when they've moved from here to there or there to here and want to record the journey, not when they haven't moved at all.

I know the shape of the narrative of the kind of thing I'm writing. I love Thomas Merton's *Seven Story Mountain* and VH1's *Behind the Music.* You start down the road, you have a bad time, and in the fourth act you find redemption. You refer to the bad times but you don't mention specifics. I had a wild time, you say; I was confused. Then you have a mystical experience, and you change your life as a result of what you've seen. I know that the narratives I'm talking about were written after the fact, to put a felt experience into the context of one moment following another in time, to weave it into the fabric of a life so that it takes, becomes a true conversion, a moment that changes everything. I've spent my life avoiding mystical experiences, but my hope is that the arc of the narrative will take over if I throw myself into it, and after that point I will know some things with some slow certainty, that

I will live the second half of my life without anxiety, in the beatific peace of the devout.

Why would you want to listen to me? I'm only speaking to myself. But I have this feeling that beneath that protoplasmic bit of flesh you carry around with you, in that private world you carry deep inside of you, the one composed of words, you might understand me, that maybe you feel unhinged as I do, as though you're watching yourself as an actor in some movie, that at some level you've been lying to everyone and you can't, for one second more, sustain it. You want to look out through your eyes and speak with your own voice. You feel as though you're always lying, and you're sick to death of lying, of the almost-true, of advertising, of inauthenticity. The devil has many tools in his toolbox, according to Oscar Wilde, who should know about duality, and the handle that fits all of them is the lie.

I may choose to leave things out as I write this, but I'll try very hard not to lie.

I'm a boring person. I live a block away from the house where I grew up. I teach at the college my parents went to. My daughter took dance lessons from my kindergarten teacher. My son had my middle-school algebra teacher. I've been married for twenty-five years.

Of course, things have changed around me. My suburban neighborhood is now an island bordered by interstate superhighways built to get the new suburbanites sixty blocks away. I now live within the city.

When I was a child I went to church each Sunday and learned the catechism, and neither one of my children has been more than once or twice. My son was baptized in the church, and my daughter was baptized with a water hose in my mother's backyard, and it's all been because of indecision. My children's childhood has gone by like a freight train, and every Sunday, *every single one,* I've had the Ash Wednesday experience of feeling as though we should be doing something and then not doing it. And if we were to go someplace, it wouldn't feel right—too this, too that. Uninteresting mostly. I want fervor but am frightened of it. I hate it when words are ugly or illogical or insincere, but who am I to judge this—all these good people—and I get in these internal battles with myself and don't go back.

Still I don't give it up entirely, and always, every Sunday, I have this feeling that I've left the house and the water is running from some faucet, some burner still glowing red-hot on the stove, as though I should go back. I could live forever, knowing me, in this non-state. I'm a patient person, indecisive, slow and sluggish as a drainage ditch, a bad combination of qualities.

So I have high hopes for this project, this jump-start of spirituality, but so far Lent has become, like Christmas, a time for shopping. Except I seem to buy myself gifts. For instance, I had an extra hour on the third day of Lent, and I was in my car and went to the new hardware store to buy a wastebasket for my son's room, but they didn't have any, so I ended up in the old mall—a different mall, it seems, on each new day of Lent.

In the first upscale mall, I felt upscale. The second was even newer and more upscale, and I felt new and purchased the fragrance of Norway.

But the third mall was the one from my childhood—the old people's mall, my daughter calls it (my daughter, who has said that when she dies she wants to be reincarnated as a mall, and she points euphorically to each of her limbs—Nordstrom's here and Jacobson's here and Lazarus here and Parisian there), and in every reflective surface at the old people's mall I saw this old woman rising up toward me, and I felt her already residing in every cell.

How do you put blush on sagging cheeks? Where does eye

shadow go when the lids are hooded? The texture of my hair is suddenly an old person's hair. How is this happening so quickly— in just three days it's happened—and why am I still so vain in spite of it?

The mall was old. The clothes were sale-rack things brought in from other stores; the clerks were dressed in old house dresses, stooped over, with poorly colored hair. There's a sweet ancient woman with a large goiter-looking growth on her cheek who sells the lingerie and asks if you're a member of the bra and panty club when you make your purchase. She's been there as long as I can remember. Every surface was dusted somehow with gloom, and I felt myself sinking down.

I swim through a sea of half-priced sweaters, holiday dresses with sleazy cheap lace fabrics. I spray fragrances over my new fragrance, and they have the bitter scent of alcohol, gardenia potpourris, the prom flowers that you touch once and the petals bruise. I see a rack of purses, and I realize how the one I'm carrying has become too heavy on my shoulder—if I could only lighten this load, I could fly.

A smaller purse would do it. A thinner strap. Something I can barely feel as I'm walking through what will soon be, I'm sure, an endless spring. I buy an on-sale purse and a smaller wallet to go inside, one that matches the leather. I leave the mall feeling sick that I've made another purchase, but I feel lighter, too—new fragrance and a purse. I've reinvented myself. My life is new. I've made a vow. I'll go home and write about it. I have to change my life.

A False Spring

On the fourth day of Lent I look for dining room furniture to replace the ornate pieces I inherited from my mother. They're pieces that she inherited from *her* mother. They're overcarved things that the daughter of a coal miner would have bought, pieces that look, each one of them, as though they're trying to imitate chairs that kings and queens might sit in. When I was a child, my mother kept this furniture in the basement of our house, and she stored all the Christmas wrapping paper in the buffet. The chairs were covered in gold velvet.

Once she moved them out of the basement and covered the chairs in red. She gave me her simple Duncan Phyfe. But when my mother died eight years ago, I inherited the old set and felt some responsibility for it.

I have to explain that my dining room used to be my favorite room. It gets the late afternoon sun, and when we bought the house it was papered with a rust-colored paper that glowed each day at four. As soon as the furniture was moved into this room, I hated all of it. I repapered the walls in a Victorian print. I hate Victorian. So I took that paper off and painted the walls cream, then white. I re-covered the chairs in a pale blue. It looked awful. Then I papered the walls in blue and white, and it still looks awful. Something about it defeats me every time I look at it, which is, of course, all the time.

You have a perfectly good life, my insightful, wonderful son said to me once, but it's not the life you want. Where does this wisdom come from?

When my husband and I were first married, we used to entertain. Since we moved into this house, we've hardly ever done it. It's been worse since I inherited the furniture. Until I get the room right, I'm somehow ashamed of it, and even more ashamed, as I'm writing this, of how shallow I am about it. For some reason I've put some portion of my life on hold because I can't seem to get my house right.

We moved to this house in part to be closer to my mother when she was in and out of the hospital so often. It made the drive much easier. She was manic-depressive, often psychotic, and I had two young children and a full-time job. There were months when I had to take her to shock treatments or to the hospital or to a clinic to check her lithium levels or to the grocery store, and living within a mile made it possible. Shortly after we moved to this house, her illness was so bad the doctor overmedicated her while trying to bring her back. He almost killed her. She was so toxic they had her in psych intensive care, watched around the clock. She was on a locked ward to begin with, and intensive care is behind another locked door, and there are six locked rooms inside of that one, with chicken wire in the windows, like a lockdown in a prison.

I remember sitting there with her when I was a child, once before when she was that bad. I'd made a dress myself—picked out the fabric and worked more diligently than usual at getting the zipper straight and the sleeves inserted just right. I wore it to visit her in the hospital. It was the color, I remember now, of that wallpaper. She couldn't, of course, notice the dress. She was in some other world than the one that I was living in. She called intensive care the inner sanctum. That last time she was in there, she had visions of the universe exploding. It was so real to her, and her children were in the middle of it. It was an intricate vision, and when I read astronomy I see it there in supernovas and in the strangely cold and fierce Darwinian violence of the galaxies.

All her adult life, in the time woven around the worst parts of her illness, the dysthymic or non-manic/non-depressed times that create those problems of identity in the child of a manic-depressive (which parent is the real one, what is the soul), I remember her wanting to get away from here, to leave my father, to become a visionary or a saint or a great concert pianist—something other than a suburban housewife. I just wanted her to serve out her time as my mother, to bring my forgotten projects to school, to help me decorate my room, to have the meals on the table and know when I needed stockings, to notice when I'd spent hours making a dress to wear to visit her. I've written about this before and thought I'd grown past it, but as I'm writing this I think that maybe I never gave myself the time to grieve, eight years ago, at her death. Instead I took this furniture into the house in the neighborhood where I grew up and took on the most understandable parts of her illness—the shopping and the restlessness.

So I look for furniture and I look for windows—if there were more light in my house, maybe I would stay home and not, all the time, be running for the mall. There's a storm warning and hardly anyone is out, and the furniture salesmen seem to stalk me through the stores.

So there's a pattern here, no? I've so far spent Lent shopping, and it's all to lift me from this gloom I feel—the furniture that reminds me of the dead, the room that doesn't let in light.

There's a blizzard coming, according to the weathermen. They stand outside in front of a mobilecam in Greenwood and Noblesville, in Lafayette and Bloomington, human barometers. Is it here yet? Do you feel it, Joe? Oh yes they do, say the poor souls standing by the interstate, their hair blowing off their bald spots; they've felt the temperature shift two degrees at least, and the color of the air has darkened. The men and women in the newsroom scan the radars; they show Doppler scanners pulsing with orange and green.

I feel a slight shift toward the Doppler blue, a star rushing toward us two degrees colder. It will break down into icy bits, the star, and fall all over us.

Blue shift. Red shift. I love astronomy. Once I read that spectrographic lines of light from distant galaxies look exactly like piano keys, and I thought about the music of the spheres. Now and then something like that will astonish me, but it has to be that big.

— — —

In the afternoon, I went to the Flower and Patio Show at the fairgrounds, crab apple trees in bloom and tulips and azaleas and daffodils and creeping phlox and magnolia and rhododendron. I'm so excited, I say, as we're walking toward the pavilion, and I remember the initial thrill of early marriage years, the possibility when you saw the landscaped gardens that you too could duplicate Eden.

Back when I didn't know a single name for a single flower, nothing was more exciting than to discover those names and press the flower in my memory. What is this tree? What kind? Does it bloom? What color are its leaves in fall? Could we truly attract those birds, could we make a terrace out of that material? What is it? Bluestone? What a lovely name, and I could buy it and make my yard into an extension of my house, burying those lovely stones in sand and planting marigolds and sitting on these vinyl/metal chairs with blue plastic glasses filled with ice and sugared tea.

We could build that deck, that playhouse, that screened-in porch. That pond is filled with what? With goldfish, koi—another lovely word. Forsythia? You can force them when winter is too poisonous. Hummingbirds will come to flowering tobacco or sugar water. It was so amazing, all of it. You buy a house, and you can buy a bucket of paint in a whole spectrum of colors—flowers, metals, rocks, and sunsets. Wallpaper, wheat paste, garden tools, different kinds of saws. A china pattern, kitchen glasses, your own coffee cups in whatever color you choose, neighbors who come out in the sunlight and disappear at dusk, a drawer for bills, a closet with linens, white pine trees, an Irish setter, and a car— a luminous life, all ahead of you.

That's how I'd always felt about the Flower and Patio Show. But not this year. I'd seen it all before, every last planting, every possible combination of colors. It smelled of the same cinnamon-covered almonds and popcorn; there were the same familiar sounds of salesmen and vacuum cleaners.

I want desperately to take some part of spring home to my house with the dead furniture and wintry light. Those tulips? They've been cut from the bulbs, and the petals are ready to fall. Azaleas? Impossible to grow them here; I've been taken in before. It never works. The same with rhododendron. Daffodils? They've already bloomed, and there's that papery wilt near the base of the flowers. I leave with nothing.

Outside the pavilion the snowflakes are thick as slices of bread, but not from heaven. I remember them from five years ago. I remember the first time, when I was in my twenties, that I saw ice-glazed blades of grass, and they looked like Christmas tinsel. I remember the first time I really saw hoarfrost and learned that word. I was twenty-three. I'm sure all of these things were there in my childhood, but I didn't name them and so don't remember them. I remember them only from my twenties, when I began to write and so began to see and was stunned, over and over, by what I saw. The way weeds dry along old railroad beds in the fall, milkweed, goldenrod, Queen Anne's lace, bluestem, the way sycamore trees look like bolts of lightning in the winter, a skinned deer twisting from a tree in someone's yard—the commute from New Castle to Richmond in an old Corvair that drove off the road, now and then, on its own. I was amazed by the small towns, amazed by the coffee shops in particular, in the middle of winter the coffee and the eggs that I had just learned to order, just learned had names like "over easy."

When I think about those years now, I remember them intensely as the first years of my life.

They were also the first years I came to know the depression I would live with, would learn to ride like waves. How miserable I could be. How absurd it was, how absurd it *is* to think that now I remember all this crystalline joy when in the middle of it, if you'd asked me, I would have said I was more miserable than I had ever been. Why doesn't the present moment ever feel like it feels in memory? And it's not that depression colors everything, because as miserable as I often think I am, I can sit here thinking about those ice-glazed stems of grass, and the first time I noticed hay bales and tried to understand their slant, and think that that was paradise, so this moment right now when I'm thinking about those moments in that light must be paradise as well. And when I lived there, in that town, and drove each day through the country, and noticed it for the first time, I thought that paradise was driving into this very city and living where I'm right at this very moment thinking I'm so miserable. Please, Mr. Einstein, would you once again explain time to me.

On the way home from the Flower and Patio Show, the snow changes to fine hail like balls of Styrofoam. None of it amazes me, and I want more than anything for it to re-amaze me. I've seen it before, though. I saw it in just those terms then. Styrofoam.

When he was seven or eight, my son's friend Zach spent the night, and they broke a beanbag chair into pieces at three in the morning. The basement was filled, several inches of the balls along the floor. We heard the boys laughing and went down to this surreal vision of jumping boys and white balls. We gave them plastic cups to scoop the balls into trash bags, but the foam stuck to the insides of the cups with static, and in the end the cups repelled the balls. And the balls stuck to the little boys' legs and arms and clothes, and when they emerged from the basement, they brought the bits of white with them through the house, and you couldn't sweep them, and they were too coated with electrons to be sucked into the vacuum.

Confession

The fifth day of Lent is Sunday, of course, and I've vowed to, in addition to writing this, go to church. It's the same one I went to as a teenager, the one where my mother heard voices. It's a sweet service, really, a baby in a full Christening dress who pulls the glasses off the preacher's face and throws them on the floor. Don't try to see through a glass either darkly or otherwise, the baby says; I want to see your eyes, right now, in this incarnation.

My mother was crazy in this place, and I was too young to understand a bit of it, not any of it, so I was probably cruel to her, and she was very kind, always, to me. And when I went to housekeeping, as my grandmother would say, her craziness intruded on my discovery of flowers' names and learning to grocery shop and teach and have a husband. I had no time for it because my life, my time, was *time,* and she'd outlived her usefulness. When the doctors said she needed to be put away for her own good, I convinced myself that it was entirely for her good, not mine. I signed the commitment papers. She terrified me, but I feel guilty and must have felt guilty then that I didn't take her in.

What would that have meant? Perhaps a giving over of my life. She bought three condominiums in one wild manic phase. She bought two cars. She bought an entire trunkload of on-sale-after-Easter toy ornaments. Her blood pressure soared; she never slept. She went to psychics and fell in love with other manics. As it was, when she was out of the hospital and sunk down low, I would take her and my grandmother and my infant son to the grocery, buying food for three separate households, all these dependent beings hanging on to my silver cart with its awkward turning wheels. That was hard enough.

Six months after a judge refused to have her commited to

Central State Hospital, her mania spiraled out of sight. She saw the world exploding in a vision and died in her bed. All day long she lay there, her glasses by her morning coffee, and it breaks my heart to think of it. My brother and I broke into the house at night, the lights all on from morning, the radio blasting NPR. The animation in the face that had burned at too high a pitch was gone, like that. For one week afterward I knew I'd seen the soul, by its absence only. I saw it in every face I came across. For one week.

I've spent the years since her death realizing, slowly, like a photograph coming into focus, how easily I could have been kinder to her. I wouldn't tell her what I was doing; I resented every phone call because I was, I felt, her only real life, and it was too much to bear, dragging this other soul with me. She is in many ways more real and present to me since she's gone. I don't remember the illness as much as I remember her, and whatever I mean by her is I guess the soul. Which is? That quiet eternal-feeling something that's eclipsed by all the storms.

Dragging one extra soul—one, as I see in retrospect, well-loved soul who loved every cell of me no matter how sick she was. How cruel I was to her because of this, the thing that appears to be driving this document, my self-absorption.

I Am

But how do you get outside the ego?

I remember a time when I was in middle school and I tried (three in this sentence already) to stop saying "I" for a week. I'm not sure why I did that (six for the sixth day of Lent).

Now and then *one* becomes just so aware of it, hemmed in by it; one feels so selfish. In the past year, at times I'll hear my voice talking to my husband, on a Friday night, say (that night of perpetual self examination and new beginnings), and I'll hear my own voice in my ears and go I-I-I-I-I in an attempt at exorcism. But when I stop there's nothing, no content to animate this voice, nothing left to say. Aren't you bored by this incessant narrative of me? But no, he listens and continues listening to anything, my somatic symptoms, the endless parade of characters at work recounted weekly in the purple dusky light of the neighborhood bar and grill. My litany, my confessions, stories. He listens and responds and never seems to judge, the only one to ever come so far into this cage of solipsism, and still there are caverns of "I" closed off to him. I get lost in those caverns and need someone to pull me out.

Those cavities where I get lost are like the endless caves beneath the limestone in Kentucky, and you have to realize I'm terrified of the dark and caves. In the nineteenth century doctors put consumptives on shelves in the middle of those caves, keeping them from the light and air, thinking the dark dampness might cure them. That's my recurring nightmare. I feel at times like a part of my soul is dressed in a black gown and lying on a cold stone shelf in the dark.

I was twenty-one when I had the first real shudder of depression, the one that feels like something different, where you become aware of the reality of death. It lasted through the first two years of marriage, and I went through my life outside of it. You might not have known if you'd seen me. It was a shudder, truly, that would come over me whenever I would even see a postage stamp of someone who had died; it was all I thought about, and it felt like that tubucular vision. If you've experienced it, you know what I'm talking about. If you haven't, you have no idea. I've never talked to a writer who hasn't felt it. Celine said that no art was possible without a dance with death, and this is, I think, the particular dance he means.

It was, in an odd sort of way, a gift. I understood poetry. It fueled my writing. Though it made me angry, I think, at people who loved me and yet were unable to save me from it. Direct my eyes outward, take me out of this solipsism. Talk about travel and faraway places, talk about books and music and art, talk about Jung. My husband is the smartest, kindest man I know. He loves me enough to follow me into any labyrinth. I'm grateful for that. Marrying him, my grandmother said to me right before she died, is the smartest thing you ever did, and I know she's right. But this shudder, this anti-mystical experience like anti-matter or anti-gravity; at the same time I was marrying him in this world, it was the service that tied me to the world of the imagination. And how was I to reconcile these marriages, and how was I to understand this as different from the strange marriage of my mother's psyche to chaos?

Now and then I'm drawn away from him. And I want him to pull me back, to keep me grounded in the world of morning coffee and evening news. I-I-I-I-I. No one is more self-centered than a depressive. How do you get outside of it? The origin of most human evil is the inability to see other human beings as real. I've lived with him for decades, and sometimes I think I've never really seen him.

Why are we made this way, as individuals, and is that the thing we have to grow out of? Sometimes I look at my children, so much of me in them, and my husband, and I think so this is eternity, the fresher version springing up, the ones who will someday in the future learn the names for flowers. I can see, when I think about an insect that lives for a day and mates and gives birth during that day and dies, how the children are in fact the eternal on and on of that initial insect, a carbon copy, an improvement. [And I've never understood the concept of individual salvation. It has always felt to me that we're saved as a species or community or not at all. Maybe it's just the DNA that's saved, and we're simply conduits.]

So why do I feel each thing so personally? Why are we limited to these six pathetic senses when there are other dimensions and worlds that we could see and understand if there were more of them? And why do we feel pain individually within the confines of our own skin? Is it just so I can carry this DNA as long as possible and not just see the world as it really is, a constant exchange of energy, of life feeding on death? And why am I unable to feel this, to really sense this evolutionary vision of eternal life? And would I want to live forever, really, inside this "I" or any other "I," so limiting finally? The "I" can't be the thing that's in God's image, can it? Can it?

If it's just the genes that want to replicate, these things without self-consciousness, why do we have this silly sense of ourselves as individual, as worthy of notice in the cosmic scheme of things? And so do we need to learn to contain more souls than just our own? Is that what saints do, is that the lesson of all religion?

It's one o'clock, and I've wasted another day straightening the house, calling about basketball tickets, getting a collar for my dog, sitting now getting my once-a-week Greek lunch, the floor in the restaurant littered with strawpaper and feta, the nyah nyah nyah of the erotic music, the drums saying abandon all of it, let go and dance. What if I were to abandon this Protestant treadmill walking and simply were to whirl, the insistent downbeat foot down and down and down and down. If I haven't come to some conclusions or made some subtle shift or change at the end of these forty days, if I haven't somehow resurrected whatever it is that's lost—or at least found it—then I'll give up ever trying.

Housekeeping

Back in January, I began straightening my office at the college where I teach—down through the layers of job-related detritus, years and years of it. One of my cabinets had been locked for at least five years, and I'd lost the key. I had no idea what was in it, but probably some sort of secret something I thought I'd be ashamed of if the plane or car or whatever it was that was taking me somewhere I can't remember crashed. Years ago some literary magazine students moved into an office in the basement of the building and found a whole cache of love letters some professor had left behind in a desk drawer. It was January, two weeks before school started. I should have been writing, but I'd just gotten back from interviewing job candidates at the MLA in Chicago (where everyone looked, once again, like me), and I was compelled to clean out every drawer. I wanted to walk into my office and see order. I wanted to be able to find things. I wanted to throw away years of student papers and unnecessary bits of this and that. I've been known, in the past, for my chaos. I'd never once in my entire life thought of straightening this thoroughly.

But I was driven. The anteroom became filled with rows of black trash bags with hand-lettered signs reading "Trash." (It was the only way, someone told me, that the maintenance staff could tell it from my usual array of bags and clutter.)

It took me three weeks, and I worked every day. It became a stop on people's daily tour. Come see this, they'd say; you won't believe it. When I was done, I bought a green glass vase and put it in the window for the light. I bought a Pier One rug with the same green and some purple. I straightened every one of my books and put things into files—correspondence, advisees, EN 4this and 4that, drafts of earlier books. I found pieces of administrative history I'd forgotten about, a record of all these years at that place. I had signed letters from Allen Ginsberg and Doris Lessing and Russell Banks and Joyce Carol Oates all stuffed in file cabinets along with class notes and extra sanitary napkins. I put the letters in one file for the library.

I had no more idea why I was doing that than I have an idea why I'm writing this. No idea, really, though one feels oddly like a preparation for the other.

When my friend Greg came by one day and saw that I was still straightening (Greg, whose office rivals mine in disorder—though not quite as bad only because he's been here for a shorter time), he said, you know, if I were someone who didn't know you, just looking down from outer space, I'd be worried.

I know, I said, like I'm getting ready to die.

Not that, he said, but like you're getting ready for some big decision, some major change.

Like getting rid of my mother's hated dining room furniture. She never liked it either. It was her mother's. She kept it around out of the same guilt. It's like it's haunted, I said.

No, he said, and laughed. It has to be more than that.

You don't understand, I said. For me, that would be a major change.

A Well-Lighted Place

On the seventh day of Lent, I got a better start. My daughter went to school early. I made her lunch, transferred the pants she wanted to wear from the washer to the blast furnace on high, dropped her off, looked for some note cards she'd misplaced, picked up both children's clothes from their floors, picked up an orange peel from the study, put the newspapers in the recycling and the toothbrushes in their holders, let the dogs outside and back in several times, made and ate some breakfast, and got to my office in Broad Ripple by nine.

Since I started this, I write in a notebook and transfer it to a computer in this office, so I'm often two days behind. I spent the morning typing and shaping and adding as I typed, and then it was noon, and I went for a walk.

Broad Ripple is a small town that's been incorporated into the city. No buildings higher than three stories, a grid of streets lined with small shops—Birkenstocks, art galleries, restaurants and bars, dried-flower places owned by middle-aged women whose children are gone, most of the city's vintage clothing stores. Teenagers skateboard here in the summer; it's near the city arts magnet school, and people and their dogs walk up and down the railtrail connecting the village to the city and to the suburbs farther north.

I rent a room in a tiny brown-shingled gingerbread house, and there are five other freelance writers who rent space here as well. This is a new space for me, and I like it. I like that in the quiet I can hear other keyboards being tapped, that the guys get up and run together in the middle of the day, that whatever it is that saps your strength at a college or any place of business—the politics— doesn't exist here. Everyone's working on his own, and this is close to anyplace you could want to eat, and there's the trail that goes through the woods and over the city's only sluggish river, and everyone seems glad to be here. I like that there is no time wasted in meetings, that there's a direct entrepreneurial quality to things, that everyone has children, and there's not that odd elitism that so easily descends on academics. As I'm writing this, I overhear one of my officemates saying "You know, I think I charged you five hundred for the last direct mail, but if it was four hundred, that's fine too for this one." He wanted to be done with it, no haggling, because outside his office window there was a little boy named Benjamin, and he wanted to talk to him. "Benjamin," he said, and the boy said he was walking with his mother on the trail and they were going to go visit his daddy, who was a fireman.

There's a pine tree outside my window, and someone left a telescope in my office, and there are feral cats living in the backyard. To one side of us there's a law office, and to the other side and behind us there are beauty salons—Envy and Cowboys and Angels. Across the street there's a yarn store where old women knit and say archaic words like "purl" and "worsted," and sometimes they have to be convinced to unlock the door to let in a customer. Beside that there's another house filled with offices, and on the other side of that there's, I kid you not, a pet chiropractor. Broad Ripple is ground zero for hair salons and alternative therapies, and we think the chiropractor is doing some kind of pet owner primal scream therapy, because now and then we hear someone screaming primally.

Not a one of us in here is in competition with another. We have no reason to give each other a list of our accomplishments. One of us edits an arts magazine; one of us plays in an odd alternative polka band of fifteen musicians who have vowed to play this strange amalgam of ironic polka and world beat music on instruments they don't play professionally. Everyone's always handing everyone CDs and saying "You've got to hear this." Everyone is some sort of copywriter.

Yesterday they were standing in the kitchen while I was working on days five and six, and they were talking about how the music they listened to when they were teenagers—say, the Ramones—seemed so incredibly fast then, and now when they listen to it, it seems so amazingly slow. Like filmmakers from early films, all that lingering on one image, on one symbol before the camera moves on, slowly, to another one, how when you watch those films you can feel the sped-up pace of modern life churning inside of you—get on with it, get on with it, I get it, your point?

And Bergman, one of them said, I can't watch Bergman now without laughing—all that drama, *death is bad*.

My students can't stand to read *Jude the Obscure* for the same reason, the prolonged depressive agony. It strikes them as simply a Prozac deficiency. One of my students came up to me last semester and said she couldn't wait to graduate; four years as an English major, and every class it was life is meaningless and then you die and yada yada ya. And once you got out of modernism and into postmodernism, it was life is meaningless but ironic and funny and then you die. She couldn't stand it. It's like every teacher stands there, she said, class after class, getting all this joy out of saying "you will die."

Big fucking deal, she said.

My friend Andy said that the great undiscovered passion in contemporary literature is joy.

So here, the seventh day of Lent, I've been writing since nine this morning and it's after two, and a mood that began in Ash Wednesday sloth and lethargy has lifted today only because I've been writing every single day for seven days, and today my house is in order and writing is most of what I've done. Who will ever want to read this but, someday, perhaps, my family? And I don't care at all, not one bit, because the process itself is so exhilarating.

At lunchtime I went for a walk around the village, though I'd intended to walk, because of yesterday's insights, down the trail and into the woods. The things I remembered being stunned by were all things I'd seen on drives through the country. So I thought that's it, that's the change I need to make.

But of course I walked through Broad Ripple instead. I went into a handmade furniture store, where I was amazed at the plain beauty of cherry Shaker tables, and then I went to an art gallery and listened to artists talk about some crazy artist who'd been in and defaced another artist's painting. I tried to go into Eden, a nightclub in what used to be an old library, but it was locked. I looked in through the door, and the walls were sponge-painted black with a gilt mirror at the top of the first flight of stairs. So Eden was closed to me, and so, as it turns out, was the Upper Room Martini Bar, which doesn't open until seven-thirty.

It's Tuesday, and usually on Tuesdays I begin grading papers early in the morning, then spend the day stressed until the evening, when I teach a three-hour seminar which I worry about all day, and then I come home to a family in bed asleep. On the way home I stop at the grocery to buy the midweek supplies of lunch stuff that we've always gone through by Wednesday, and I usually buy a bottle of wine.

Last year on seminar night I would come home at ten and drink glasses of wine and eat junk food until I got sleepy at midnight or so. I've never been good at getting to sleep, and night classes make it impossible; I'm too revved up. So I spent last winter with Bill and Monica.

But the thing is, this Tuesday is much more joyful than any Tuesday this semester has been or will be. Would it always be like this if this were the way I spent my days?

Vocation

I'm not sure of today's date, but I know it's the eighth day of Lent. Yesterday, I'm pleased to say, I spent the day writing and didn't buy a thing, though on Monday, I neglected to report, I got an overdue check from Alabama and bought a lamp I'd coveted. Antique brass with a linen shade, it gives me pleasure.

I stopped in the Monon to get a to-go coffee and recognized the waitresses, former students. A woman with black-dyed hair and clothes and a pierced lip came out of Theo's Garden carrying a paper cone of narcissus. The old man who gives out parking tickets had a fresh supply of pink envelopes in his back pocket. Sunday there were six inches of snow on the ground, and today it's all melted. The ground is soggy but the sidewalks are dry, and the early daffodils withstood the blizzard.

I have to say that I've never trusted joy. I'm much more at ease with despair and misery, which is one of the reasons why I haven't quit my job.

And I'm a little giddy with the joy of working on this project, a project I hadn't foreseen or intended. The slogging part of it hasn't kicked in yet, but it will.

I've never trusted joy of any kind because of my mother's manias, which were far more terrifying than her despair. The despair was manageable. It took place within the house, and the mania made her unpredictable and drove her out into odd places. She got the dinners on the table, she made our beds. The muscles in her face grew somehow lax like tomatoes that had been left too long on the vine. She aged by fifteen years when she was depressed, and those same muscles lifted her face into the face of a young woman when she was manic.

It was the mania that landed her in the hospital, and there

were three different hospitals she landed in. The first one was in Ohio and was run by Seventh-day Adventists. It was a beautiful wooded place, I was told, and when she came back from that place weeks or sometimes months later, her beautiful face was moon-shaped with the weight she'd gained. We drove to Ohio a couple of times to see her at a neutral restaurant, and I vaguely remember the ride down with my father and grandmother and brother, but I don't remember any of the meetings. I was a depressive, anxious child myself, and I'm sure those meetings were painful.

The second hospital was the local Methodist-run place, the locked ward, and I went there often, with my father, to see her. The carpet was blue, and the patients went up to the counter to light their cigarettes from a common lighter. My mother was addicted to Salems. My father made us write her letters while she was in the hospital, and when she died and I cleaned out her home, I found the letters tied with a ribbon in a ceramic tile box she'd made one year in occupational therapy. Whenever she came home from the hospital, she had a box of things she'd made, like a child coming home from a year of kindergarten.

The third was the state-run hospital, and it was the place of last resort. She was never violent. (It's funny, my brother said recently, but when I think of Mom now, the thing I remember is not so much her illness but her kindness, and that's true.)

But my mother's mania was often intractable. When delirium set in, only gibberish came from her mouth. At that point she was sometimes diagnosed as schizophrenic. After a period of weeks, they couldn't keep her there. She was on, throughout her life, every possible medication. She took lithium, she took Haldol, she took Mellaril for years and years and developed that tremor in the hand. Shock treatments often worked. She did electro shock and insulin shock. Her story has been documented in other women's stories of the time. You can read them.

When she was gone, I missed her unbearably. I had no one to talk to. I wrote her letters on pink onionskin paper, and I filled them with upbeat stories about my wonderful middle-school life—which of course wasn't.

I didn't mean to write about this, I meant to write about the fear of joy. For the first thirty-five years of my life, I'd say, that was the driving force in me. Because my mother's manic side was the artistic side and the mystical side, I was afraid of that same impulse in myself. She played the piano and sang and hung out with odd people when she was spiraling out of control. And she became an odd mystic. She read sacred texts. God spoke to her. She was euphoric but never needed to be converted. She was always, at every moment, ultimately concerned with God.

Because the depressive side was the middle-class housewife side, and that was the not-crazy side, according to everyone of any authority, that was the side I clung to. So I live in the same neighborhood; I'm married to my college sweetheart; I have two children, and they go to my same high school and middle school. My children will have very few, if any, memories of me writing. I do it someplace else and talk very little about it. I'm the carpool mom. I've never once in my life been manic, but I understand it. It's my biggest terror. As is change. As is religion. Or maybe was.

Which leads me to where I want to go today. Lent lasts for six weeks, and I'm one-sixth through. If it's a journey, I'm one-sixth there, and I have no sense of destination. Since I started this on Ash Wednesday, I assume that this is some midlife something having to do with religion or perhaps with mourning.

I've never taken my children to church, and in the past few weeks both of them have mentioned it. My daughter said she wants to go to the church at the dinner theater. My son accidentally (he says) bought a CD that has Christian lyrics, and he said it made him feel weirdly better about himself. He's reading the children's Bible. So it's come up. My brother's family is devout, and they try various means to get us to church—though never obnoxiously. One of the kids is in the bell choir; would you like to come see?

I read three things today. The first was a review of a biography of Bruce Chatwin in the *Times*. All those books about the Aborigines, and he didn't interview many Aborigines. The books were dazzling but all filtered through himself, and this self was married and closeted gay. I wondered if he would have walked the Songlines if he weren't closeted, and if I would have known about them otherwise, and I have to say I'm glad I do. I wonder how much the pain of a double will gives rise to art. And how odd that none of that comes through in his work, which is nonfiction, which means that it's supposed to conform to some verifiable reality. And the reviewer says that of course the truth comes through in the fiction. In nonfiction, when the "I" is the same "I" as the one who greets the everyday world, there's often a greater slippage between what seems to be and what is. There's usually a lacuna that the nonfiction writer uses as a loom to weave the words through. A mystery revealed by biographers and fiction.

The second was an article in the paper, one of those weirdly inspiring stories about a guy who worked for an architectural firm, wore suits and ties and went to meetings he hated, and who one day for who knows what reason, he said, put down his pen and walked outside. "Disgusted with everything, I guess," he said in the paper. "I needed some fresh air."

His walk took him to a toy train store in Union Station. The trains brought back all these childhood memories in clangs and whistles, and he spent an hour or more talking to the owner, and then he borrowed some videos to watch at home.

He watched those videos for the rest of the day. And he stayed home from work the next day to watch them, and then the next day and the next. For three days he watched toy train videos.

"Another day goes by and I'm still watching train videos," he was quoted in the paper as saying. "I was captured with trains and I'm still not sure why."

He started buying train cars then, and he set them around the house just so he could look at them. He still didn't know why.

Somehow the obsession helped him quit his job, and he started freelancing. He designed some redevelopment strip malls, and in the process he suggested an idea for a train-theme restaurant, which got him talking to Lionel Trains, which had just been bought by Neil Young, who liked the idea and invited the man out to his ranch in California, and before you knew it the man was hired to design all the new Lionel trains and complete systems with houses and trees and bridges and fences and people, these miniature worlds.

Which he does in a small house in a small town in Indiana, and he never wears a suit. He works for himself. He spends each day designing toy train cars. It still makes him happy to look at them.

I loved that story because it's irrational and it's redemptive.

That story is a midpoint story, a forty-five-year-old's story. The basic conflict was set early on, and there are things the protagonist desires and obstacles in his way, and he makes compromises and tries to live with the conflict and could go on that way forever and ever amen, but *something happens,* and the whole thing comes to a head right smack dab in the middle of the book. Midpoint.

Pick up any extended narrative, a novel or biography, say, and see how many pages there are. Divide that number in half and turn to the center of the book. Someone dies or something major happens.

Which brings me to the third thing I read today.

That copy of Augustine's *Confessions* I picked up a week ago? I've been reading it. Every night, a few more pages.

In my twenties I would have approached a book like this with major fear and trembling. I would circle around it in the library, maybe pick it up, but think to myself no, put that back, this is a major crazy-maker. Still, at some point I picked up *The Cloud of Unknowing*, and at some point I took a course in mysticism, and at some point I read Julian of Norwich, though I've never, I'm ashamed to say, read the New Testament. I've never wanted to have a conversion experience. If I were struck on the road to Damascus, I'd probably feel the need to check myself into a hospital. I don't trust that sort of thing.

So I'm reading St. Augustine, and I feel toward him the way I feel toward my most confused young male students. I feel motherly. Poor thing. Why put yourself through all this torture? Though for a conversion book, its strong suit seems to be logic. There are long, gorgeous syllogisms in the first part of the book, where he's trying to rationally break away from the Manichaean heresy—an idea which was comforting for someone who felt himself to be a sinner in the same way that Jungian philosophy comforts the adulterer. There are powers and forces in the world— archetypal forces in the one case, the war between matter and spirit, between good and evil, in the other—that are beyond anyone's control. In the Manichaean universe, there's a struggle between the divine light and the evil darkness of material exist- ence, and evil is independent of human free will.

I'm impressed by the intellectual rigor, by his attempts to have his imagination fasten on an image that will encompass his vision of God, so that he knows what it is he's believing in when he says that he believes. He takes up and rejects images: "So also did I endeavor to conceive of Thee," he writes. "Life of my life, as vast, through infinite spaces, on every side penetrating the whole mass of the universe, and beyond it, every way, through unmeasurable boundless SPACE; so that the earth should have Thee, the heaven have Thee, all things have Thee, and they be bounded in Thee, and Thou bounded no where. For that as the body of this air which is above the earth, hindereth not the light of the sun from passing through it, penetrating it, not by bursting or by cutting, but by filling it wholly: so I thought the body not of heaven, air, and sea only, but of the earth too. . . ." He realizes then, though, that the body of an elephant would contain more of God than the body of a sparrow, and so he rejects this image.

He conceives of himself as dust and ashes, pitiable by God. He conceives of God as Light Unchangeable. "Not this ordinary light, which all flesh may look upon, nor as it were a greater of the same kind, as though the brightness of this should be manifold brighter, and with its greatness take up all space. Not such was this light, but other, yea, far other from all these. . . . He that knows the Truth, knows what that Light is; and he that knows It, knows eternity. Love knoweth it."

"Thou art my God," he writes, "to Thee do I sigh night and day. And I said, 'Is Truth therefore nothing because it is not diffused through space finite or infinite?' And Thou criedst to me from afar; 'Yea verily, I AM that I AM.'"

Flesh both is and is not. It is because it's made by God and is not because it's finite. Only God is because unchangeable. It's the argument of contingent beings and a necessary being. I am that I am.

I sort of get it, though I don't. I don't get why a necessary being is in fact necessary. And I don't get the conflict that gives rise to the torture in this book.

So I read a biography and find out that Augustine loves women, and women seem to reciprocate the feeling. And in order to follow God truly, he feels as though he needs to become celibate, which, if we read between the lines of this text, he has not been since childhood.

So he wants to change, but please, he says, just not quite yet. He has a mistress. The mistress loves him. She isn't a character in this book. She's barely mentioned. She isn't seen.

So we have the conflict, and the stakes are high, and he feels that those stakes are high, and there's the push and pull that goes on for pages. A conversion will save his life. Without one, he will lose it.

At the beginning of this book, Augustine is a professor of rhetoric. It's like he's his high school valedictorian, the one who graduates magna cum laude from college, the one who gets a PhD and is a Rhodes Scholar, the one whose fame begins to spread.

He's a great rhetorician, and I'm pulled into his story; and then right smack dab in the middle of the book, at midpoint, he's converted.

Of course he knew when he began writing this that he was telling the story of his conversion, and as a rhetorician he knew what to say as well as how to say it. He knew that if he was writing a three-hundred-page book, the story of the conversion should come on page one-fifty, and it does. I don't know what to make of this, and I'm somehow cynical at this screenplay technique in the middle of a medieval mystery text, and this is what a crummy person I am. Cynical at St. Augustine. *St.* Augustine. I'm a cynical Midwestern woman obsessed with dining room furniture and angry at a neighbor for putting out a sign with the Ten Commandments. There's absolutely no hope for me.

Inside This Skin

I have to admit, I like him better after the conversion. Though it may be that I'm learning, as I go, how to read him. My anger at the midpoint was showing off. If you're an American at the beginning of the twenty-first century, you think you know everything there is to know, when in fact we're clearly living in the dark ages. There's hardly anything a physicist has said about time that wasn't said by Augustine in the fourth century, and more simply.

And I seem to be drawn, right now, to quitting-your-job stories, which this is. When he's converted, he wants to spend his time in contemplation. He's a writer, not a teacher. He decides to quit his job as a rhetoric professor at the end of the term. "Not tumultuously to tear" from it, "but gently to withdraw, the service of my tongue from the marts of lip labor: that the young, no students in Thy law, nor in Thy peace, but in lying dotages and law skirmishes, should no longer buy at my mouth arms for their madness."

I love it. No more *this needs a little more detail,* no more *I can't see it,* no more *what's at stake in this story,* no more *you really need to turn something in before the end of the semester if you want to pass,* none of it. No longer selling arms to the young to feed their madness. When he goes back into the classroom to finish out the year, he has some sort of hysterical bronchitis. He can't talk. Like the designer of toy diesels, he really wants to leave his daily job.

That said, the lacuna in this confession is his mistress and their children. The sons appear once, and he seems proud of them, though they were, he says, conceived in sin. He's upset by the fact that at night he dreams of her, and of other women as well. His son is sixteen, the same age as my son. All the way through, I'm dazzled by the saint's mind but looking for a hint of the woman's face, the texture of her skin, her clothing, the room she occupies, her relationship with her children and their father, her jealousy at his other lovers, perhaps relief when, finally, he forsakes all of them and becomes a priest. It's the way I felt reading Matthiesen's *The Snow Leopard,* which I also was dazzled by, whenever I remembered that he was risking his life on snow-covered mountains searching for wisdom while his young son, who had just lost his mother as his father had lost his wife, was staying back in the States with friends. I could never understand this, how you could leave your children. And of course I'm aware, as I'm typing this, that that is exactly what my mother did.

That said, I'm in awe, as I read Augustine, of what the human mind is capable of, how far it can penetrate mysteries.

Augustine is not a mystic. He's a logician, and he takes his logic like a dentist's pick jabbing at a tooth. Why this? What is this? Why not this? If this, then this? And how so? And what if? "Courage my mind," he writes, "and press on mightily. . . . Press on where truth begins to dawn." For instance: "See how the present time, which alone we found could be called long, is abridged to the length scarce of one day. But let us examine that also: because neither is one day present as a whole. For it is made up of four and twenty hours of night and day: of which, the first hath the rest to come; the last hath them past; and any of the middle hath those before it past, those behind it to come. Yeah, that one hour passeth away in flying particles."

"What is that which gleams through me, and strikes my heart without hurting it; and I shudder and kindle? I shudder, inasmuch as I am unlike it; I kindle, inasmuch as I am like it. It is Wisdom, Wisdom's self which gleameth through me; severing my cloudiness which yet again mantles over me, fainting from it, through the darkness which for my punishment gathers upon me."

If the past exists only in the present, in my memory, and the future in my perception of causality, also in the present, then my perception of yesterday is in the present as well. Yesterday, as I lived it, was without pattern, but today the pattern is clear to me. What is eternally present is my perception of pattern.

I'm writing this knowing that it's a midpoint document, midpoint in my life if I'm very lucky, midpoint in my career, beyond midpoint in the raising of my children. I know, for instance, that if I keep working on this at the same rate at which I've begun, I'll have two hundred fifty pages by Easter. I know that something will have to change around page one twenty-five, and I'm terrified to get there. As I'm writing this as it unfolds, and not in retrospect, I have no idea whether I'll reach the end and realize that nothing happened. I refuse to go on in this muddled fashion, this inauthentic thing I call my life. By the end I hope to change something, if only my dining room furniture, or to become resigned to keeping it as it is.

Yesterday I was thrilled with mysticism. It started with the train guy. Those trains were a religious experience. Those trains changed his life. They were eternally present, those toy trains.

I wanted more than anything in the world for something like that to happen, oh please oh please, to me today. I wanted to be so sure of something without thinking that I'd go out into the world and be led to something against my very will. Who cares if it was Lionel trains. It could be Birkenstock shoes or yo-yos or two-by-fours or crosscut saws. Anything, dear God, just let me be pushed by some internal or external force; let it be real and powerful and true.

So this morning there was a ninety percent chance of rain, and after several days of perfect weather it began raining and hasn't stopped. One of those days, gray and gloomy, that cast you in upon yourself. This is the story of how crazy it made me, and how I wasted an entire morning:

Yesterday I had to look up the Indiana Historical Society in my address book, and I couldn't find it under I (it was under H), but there, on the page for I, I'd written "Iconography." Since it was the day I'd read about the man who was wooed by trains, I thought I should probably follow this thread, and so I called Mother Catherine.

The number for the Rublev school rings at the St. Seraphim bookstore attached to the Joy of All Who Sorrow Church down by the Humanities Council (which is also under H). When Mother Catherine answered, she was sitting on a step with a cordless phone, reading the *Mother Earth News*. I found out that the bookstore wasn't open this week because there were services every day. I had been nursing this hope that reading St. Augustine made me ready to go back to class and paint a stroke or two, but she said that classes wouldn't begin again until after the Great Lent was over. She asked if I'd made a vow and if I was keeping it, and I said I was.

I thanked her and got off quickly. So, I thought, since the pattern of yesterday was hoped-for mysticism, maybe I should go to one of the services. Of course it would have been too easy to call and find out when one was, or to ask Mother Catherine when I had her on the phone, but I assumed that one would probably be at twelve o'clock for a variety of reasons, including the fact, I'm embarrassed to say, that it would be the most convenient time for me, and I was trying to learn to trust, Shaker-like, in where the spirit led me. I was hoping it would lead me to something old and medieval, filled with ancient chanting and anachronism, with praying women not being replaced by younger ones at the rate at which they were dying.

Though first I had to get my daughter off to school, to make her lunch and breakfast and straighten the morning chaos in the house. On the way to school, we passed the roly-poly twin boys we pass every morning, and I smiled at how cute they were, as I always do, and this morning my daughter smiled too—it was a good day—and told me how they were in all her classes, that the teachers called them Sam and Tom because their names were really long and unpronounceable, and how they answered every question together.

She'd brought a CD to listen to in the car, and she put it in the player—some teenage girls with angelic voices singing about love—and she told me how they were going to call themselves M&M because their names both began with M, but then another singer came along called Eminem first, and they had to change their names to M2M.

I see, I said, happy that it's an easy enough morning that we can talk like this. As we get near her school, she ejects the CD and puts it in the case, then takes one of my CDs—Bonnie Raitt—and puts it in for me. I haven't asked her to do this, and it almost makes me cry, it's such a lovely thing for her to do. You have to understand, she's a thirteen-year-old. She spends an hour each morning on her hair, and she still calls me mommy in front of friends. She makes my heart swell and break and swell and break and swell, as does my son.

The middle school she goes to is the same one I went to when I was her age. I drop her off at the door and remember my mother dropping me off in just this way. My daughter and I like the same fragrances; we share bottles of Clinique Happy and now, the national fragrance of Norway. When I was her age, my mother and I liked Imprevu. Mothers and daughters are tied like this, and it will be as difficult for her to break away from me and return as it was for me.

Don't forget the rubber bands, she said, and before I went downtown to my shameful secret mystical rendezvous, I went to Osco to get supplies. I am, several days a week, my family's procurer. When I pick her up at five-thirty, she wants to braid her hair, and my son wants a protein shake because he's building his body.

When I'm done, I begin to drive, down the hill and past the house where I grew up. Maybe I'm supposed to be there, I think. Maybe I should be sitting in front of that house writing right now, and all sorts of certainties would occur to me.

I get to the light where I have to turn left or keep going straight to go downtown, and I keep going straight. I'm heading for that church.

I drive through town, past a store with a handmade sign marked "Oddities." I pass a store with a handmade sign marked "Peace." I pass storefront church after storefront church. I pass an old church that's been converted into a business college. Finally I make it to the Joy of All Who Sorrow.

I knew the neighborhood. Several years earlier I'd interviewed a man named Kevin who lived in a second-floor apartment across the street. He was dying of AIDS. I sat in on a writing class he was in at the Damien Center, a Catholic church–supported center for men and women with HIV. I'd interviewed Kevin and another man in the class, a former minister named Herb. All their lives, they'd wanted to write but hadn't. Other things, including denial, took most of their time. Aquinas said that the reason God made death is to give us a deadline. Now the knowledge of their own certain death was giving them a sense of urgency.

I have pages of notes on both of them, and I'd never written their essay. They had told me their stories, trusted me with them, and thought I would pass them on. Mea culpa. Mea culpa. I'd gotten busy with my own other things and had forgotten about them. And as I looked for a place to park near the Joy of All Who Sorrow Church, I still didn't think about them, not really. It's only as I'm writing this that I'm remembering all of it—the notes, the unwritten essay, their words and faces.

Outside the church, I had more immediate things to think

about, things that exist in Time. I walked through the rain wondering how to fasten the hood of my raincoat around my hair, wondering where to find an unlocked door in the decaying church. There wasn't a single entrance that I could find into the Joy of All Who Sorrow. Not one. Peeling paint on the large white doors and round brass locks the size of oranges. The stained-glass windows were covered over with dusty Plexiglas to protect them. Where were the nuns? Not in the bookstore; they hadn't unlocked any of the doors. They were back inside, where they were probably praying for all of us out here on the sidewalk having no idea how to get inside.

All the way to my writing place in Broad Ripple, I laughed at myself. A rainy day and I'd wasted the morning. What did I expect? There were no real synchronicities; nothing invisible spoke to me, and would I even want it to? I don't want mysticism. If any Holy Spirit were to descend, I'd want it to be quietly, subtle as a well-oiled lock or, better yet, tumblers falling into place, a drawer that fits so perfectly that when it closes it descends a fraction of an inch to keep it from flying out during earthquakes. The movement of a craftsman, the leap of the mind moving backward between today and yesterday.

So I sit down and begin telling this story, and in the middle of telling it, and only in retrospect, I remember Kevin and Herb and their friends Tim and Roy. And suddenly I'm ashamed that I'd forgotten them.

Little by little, they come back to me. The last time I saw him, Roy was the color of cigarette ash. His lover had just died. Roy was now dead as well, I'd heard. Kevin died a year ago. The woman who taught the class had called to tell me. Herb? I had no idea whether he was alive or dead. Tim was gone, I knew—the man who had walked around the house wearing his lover's cologne after he died. I look up on the shelf above my computer, in the office I'd so maniacally cleaned two months before, and there were the notes I'd taken when I talked to them. Silenced voices. Doors leading to the joy of all who sorrow. I open my notebook, and their voices rush out at me.

In Memoriam

KEVIN

Tortured crocus
you came up too early
your yellow center exposed, I don't expect you to live.
Surprise me in March. Blast the air with your stupid Mouth.
Let me see you open up at the foundation of my house.
—Kevin Cole

I went to school at Indiana University. One of my best friends, my first lover, was from New York. I was always intrigued by it.

I knew I had a job in Wabash as a buyer for an antique business, but I went to New York. I had a patron when I was there. He was rich. He had more money than God.

When I was a child, I lived in a small town, in a neighborhood of old women. I'd mow their grass and they'd give me a teapot instead of money.

I started collecting carnival glass, and I became impassioned about it.

I don't, of course, have much sentiment with stuff anymore. Now I just do it for a living. The virus has made me more minimal. I've sold a lot of what I had, just kept a few of my favorite pieces. I have a brother who's my sole heir, and he could give a shit about any of the stuff. He likes basketball, has a big-screen TV.

But back then I loved being a collector. When I had another job, I was still passionate about it. The whole concept was amazing to me, how objects come and go. I went to auctions once a week. The people at auctions are sometimes very primitive; they were shocked by me. Once I went up to a gurney to inspect this tambourine and started dancing. I went clear backward with the tambourine. I got myself into positions that were very severe, and no one could believe it.

When I first moved to New York, I ran a property-rental business. Twenty-five thousand square feet, and by God it was organized. Teapots were with teapots.

I liked the movie people best. They would come in and say "We're doing a movie set in 1948." People would rent picture frames, vanity items. We rented linens like crazy. I always thought that place would be fabulous for a play. The characters were already there. My assistant manager was a serious coke addict. He'd get paranoid. The whole five-year period was so surreal.

I loved the anonymity of New York. I could have gone out in my pajamas. Though holidays were real tough for me. I had a lover for the last two and a half years I was there. I went into the relationship very pessimistic. He was twenty-one and I was thirty-one. I knew he would leave me eventually. After two and a half years he got restless, and I understood it. We were living together then and splitting the rent.

So there was the breakup; my job ended; my patron died. I always wanted to start my own business. I'd lost a couple of good friends to AIDS then. I'd watched the process with Steve, my first lover. He was so beautiful. People would stop him on the street and give him their phone numbers. It was hardest for him to lose his looks.

For a while I was going every day. A group of his friends met for coffee and then would go to the hospital. I went one time to see him when he was in a convulsion. The IV had come out; blood was splattering around the room.

After that I went back one more time. He took my hand and said "If you really love me, you'll kill me."

There was a trip we'd planned once to go to Puerto Rico. He was delirious. He sat up in the bed and said "Get my clothes, let's do this. Now. Let's go."

I'm so horrified of getting to that point, where I'm not self-sufficient. I have no qualms about suicide. I don't really have any family. Even though I'm not, I feel sometimes like I'm really old . . . like all my friends are gone.

At this time I was still HIV-negative.

When I moved back here, I thought I was safe, but I spiraled out of control. I got this tawdry job. The great irony is I got the virus when I came back here. The disease was hardest at first, because I'm so self-absorbed. It's almost like I was jealous of it. I'm all "me me me" and this was "it it it." I couldn't escape it.

So what is this thing that was pushed into me? What is love? This whole animal nature thing, I don't get it. So what is love? Can you explain it?

I've spent the last few months of my life mesmerized with nothing. I constantly oscillate between lethargy and urgency, between doing nothing and doing everything.

But I want to spend time on the poetry. I want to write about the HIV. There's so much emotion surrounding it. My own refusal to grieve. It's hard to acknowledge a terminal illness when you don't have any symptoms yet. It's so easy to deny it.

I read this book by Thomas James. Listen to this:

The moon has gone a little sour for us
I am aware of your body and its dangers
I spread my cloak for you in leafy weather
Where other fugitives and other strangers
will put their mouths together.

And this:

With the velvet at my knees
And the silverware shining on the altar
And the stained glass moving out of focus
And the cross veiled in black,
I am present for the news of an enormous death.

I've never been afraid of death. I'm intrigued by it, in fact. I found my mother dead at fourteen. I heard her gasping for air. When the white men came and took her, I remember looking at her and thinking it wasn't her at all. I felt like her spirit left and only the shell of the body was there. It could have been anybody's body. I was so neutralized. My sister-in-law came and took my hand and said "Oh, you'll feel better about it."

There's a part of me that's a mystic. I like the idea of reincarnation. I'm fascinated by lots of different religions. If I had to declare a religion, it would be American Indian. I feel closest to God when I'm in nature. At least three times a month I take major hikes. I relate flowers more with my mother. Geraniums and petunias.

I've had many unexplainable moments in the woods. I felt Steve's presence and a boyfriend who was killed in a car wreck. Those four people. It's no question that they're out there. It's not in a particular thing.

I'd like to think that the spirit moves around a lot. I'd like to think that it doesn't just sit in a chair.

I've never been particularly religious, though. I lost a lot of my faith when my mother died. I thought if there was a

God, why did he do this to her? I was going to take my mother away and make her finally happy.

Once she stayed up all night before the 4H fair helping me glue and pin the broken antenna of a cockroach. Can you imagine it? A cockroach.

Once I bought a French china clock. And there was a polymorphous moth. I reached for the moth and the clock broke. She spent two days gluing it back together for me. She—my mother—*was* love. She never once got mad at me. Her death changed me as a person. I was shy. I didn't have friends, never got a B in my life. I never felt that I needed friends. I had my mother. Every Saturday we went to the sweet shop and had a hot fudge sundae.

Being raised like I was—Bible school and church—I told myself that at best I was bisexual. I figured that I would never act on any of it. I never saw my parents touch each other.

But I've never had sex with a girl. I didn't really have my first sexual experience until I was twenty. Even then we were all calling ourselves bisexual, not gay. I was horribly persecuted in the dorms at IU. They threw furniture at me.

Even to this day I'm not all that comfortable in crowds of gay people. So many of them are so superficial, fashion-conscious, so into money. I occasionally go to gay bars.

But I chose to adopt the Janis Joplin thing of get it while you can. I purposely choose people for sex. I know that's all it's going to be. I'm attracted to ex-cons. I like the primitiveness of these people. I like to hear their stories. People who've been in prisons, who've killed people. It's a lot more interesting than talking about Nietzsche. The danger element intrigues me.

Last summer I was really bad. I became really fascinated with prostitutes. There were men dressed up as women,

women dressed up as men. I couldn't stop. What's frightening is all these kids. They think that they're immortal. I'm really angry that they introduced this as a gay thing. Now there isn't even a group to support you.

I can't feel blame per se. I think there was a period after I first found out when I wanted to point the finger. I'm as concerned about people going through it with me. But I've had sex and haven't told them I'm positive. I know how horrible Steve felt; that experience, as traumatic and awful as it was, it didn't stop me. Listen to me. I've had sex and haven't told them I was positive. What's wrong with me?

Poetry is the thing I want to leave when I'm gone, but I don't write. I can't get myself to type up the poems I've written. If poetry is the thing I want to leave the world, I ask myself now, then why don't I focus on it? It's the most important thing to me, and still I don't focus on it. I put it off now because I'm waiting for symptoms, and still I don't have any. And so I wait.

HERB

I have to look at it from now backward.

There's always been a struggle over issues like God and goodness, almost anything dual. I loved questions like what is art, how that contrasts with religion.

I remember feeling very aware in college—religion there was very progressive. I felt in the right place because the year I began, they dedicated the new chapel. The implication is that knowledge is something that lifts you up spiritually—statues of Leibniz and Luther—neo-enlightenment. Then my struggle was made more painful because I wasn't well defined myself.

I expected that I would be able to—I knew that I had a very solid sense of values and a very Catholic view of life. It was hard to get beyond idealism and to live in the real world and be a real person.

After I left my career, I hung over the fire for a year. I needed to have a stronger sense of who I was.

I wasn't open to conversion experiences because I loved the endless process. Now I can see that it was all a search for the beginning of who I was. I was trying to be learned and skilled when I've always been more intuitive.

The weird thing about the virus is how completely all-absorbing it is to us and to our friends, and how completely invisible it is to those outside. It's like being isolated from the real world, and every once in a while you see it from outside, as someone else might see it, and it hits you again how surreal it is to be living inside this world where everyone around you is dying, where you go to funerals every week, and it's like you're on the other side of a dark glass and no one can see you. Most of the time it's not odd to us is what I'm saying. And that's what's so unbelievable about it.

Maybe that's why it seems so much larger than life. So global, constant, bigger than God.

I was a Lutheran minister, you know, before this happened. I was gay, and I had to hide it, and then after a while I didn't and I quit the ministry. For a while I went completely crazy, but then somehow I've come back to it, the ministry, but in a different way. I keep up the garden around a Lutheran church. I garden every day until I'm tired. I do this during the week, and for the most part I stay away on Sundays. I think about the church and about this illness and the friends I've lost, and I grieve because something great and important is missing in human affairs. I guess what I would call it is justice—in the Judeo-Christian context, justice is . . . shalom . . . peace . . . righteousness and peace have kissed each other. It doesn't have anything at all to do with making up for errors. There are no guarantees. Shalom means "may everything be as it ought to be." It's reconciliation.

Everyone's job is to work at relationships and to find the place where we serve each other. If anything, AIDS has taught me that life is significant when you're engaged with other people. Mourning together and encouraging together. Those simple things.

My first job after quitting the ministry was teaching art. One of my basic assumptions was that not everything is perfect, which meant that there were more possibilities.

Anyway, I overchallenged myself. I let myself be in very risky and dangerous situations, religiously and intellectually. If there's a preferred idea, I didn't care. What I did was expose myself to things. I could think of all the things I could be, but when it came to making a choice, I couldn't do it. So I did it all. I always thought that we blindly accepted these limitations to knowledge.

I had a penchant for natural religion, and the Lutheran church was very doctrinaire.

A lot of my theology was filtered through music.

My grandfather was my hero when I was a child. He was an orphan, was sent out to be on his own. He had to work his way up. He worked in a steel mill carrying slag carts that you had to dump. Then he had a career as an insurance agent.

My mother was blinded when she was young, and she accepted it as a punishment—for not being where you're supposed to be, doing what you're supposed to be doing.

Just when I was doing a lot of work and finally becoming reconciled to me, it's like I was blinded too. One thing I've learned in my treatment is what letting go is. I learned in my childhood to do without.

I'm a wanderer, someone who hasn't arrived or who arrives only to discover that nothing is there.

When things keep being senseless and you keep going, you learn something new. If I'm learning something new, then I can't decide prematurely that things don't make sense. God, I've had a hard time learning to let things be.

If there's anything I remember being, it's happy writing. I'm a poet. It was a mystery how you could be a poet without writing words, but I was. My poetry was expressed in gardening, in movement. I still have a problem with living in my mind instead of doing it. There are a lot of people writing very personal, very soul-ful writing.

Recovery and redemption are very close in meaning. It means that there is some previous state we return to. I'm very interested in Michael Fox, and one of his ideas is "original blessing." One of Luther's was "original sin." Original blessing is prior to the sin, where God says that it's all good.

There are a lot of distortions in religion. That's where a lot of the energy comes from. We're gifted. We're blessed. What we do is receive. The most appropriate response is to be grateful and explore what it is that we've received.

I like people who have facets. I hate to use "diamond" because diamonds are symbols of self-glorification. Industrial diamond, facets are able to cut through. I don't like it when people say they're dazzled. I'd rather they say we have something to talk about. Being dazzled is another way of pushing me away. The place of art is to build community and to help people see the gifts that they are. It's a language, and language is used to connect. Soul means being connected with the all.

As you can see, I'm a mystic, but I'm not a disciplined mystic. As soon as I got into seminary, the writing stopped. And I'm not a disciplined musician.

But I am a mystic. It's the world that's the sinkhole for me. My role is not defined now as a minister or as a family member or as a home builder. Celibacy is a way now of clearing things so I'm more definable, not de-focused.

When I was in high school, I wanted to be an interior designer, to make space available to actors. The enormous space that I saw was inside, but I AM in it. There was always this sense of plainness and simplicity that was not compatible with what I remember as my attempts to be sophisticated and worldly.

People perceived me as being worldly when I was simple. I wanted to do both. I didn't see the necessity to choose.

Not very often anymore, but I've always had this urge to run across a field and jump into the air. I know why cats like looking down off of shelves.

Remember what Tim said in class? He said he'd always thought the world made sense. A shining city on the hill, the New Jerusalem. And at the bottom is me, he said, and I'm crying tears of lamentation.

The ninth day of Lent, and I spent it typing up these stories. Their voices were silenced once by themselves, twice by death, and a third time in a notebook on my shelf. I'm sure now that I headed to the Joy of All Who Sorrow because something in me needed to remember them. Mea culpa. Mea culpa. I've wasted so many of my days.

St. Augustine

Starting this in anger at myself on Ash Wednesday, I thought it would have something to do with religion. Clearly, so far, it hasn't. What have I learned in the first ten days, one-quarter of the way through Lent, that I didn't know when I began?

I threw myself into yesterday thinking I would have some profound experience that would change my heart, and of course it wasn't the experience I anticipated; and just at the point when I thought it was hopeless, I came into this office one more time, as I promised myself I'd do every day until Easter, and in that process itself the change happened. Day after day, year after year, as I'm confronted with students who think they want to write but can't get started, I tell them to trust the process, and I haven't trusted it myself. When the voice inside me says look there, under that rock, I should always turn it over and see what's underneath and know that whatever it is may not be exactly what I expect or want, but will be in fact exactly what I need. Why should that be? Maybe our brains are hardwired to want to make connections and patterns out of chaotic experiences. Maybe it's nothing more than that simple material reason, all we can possibly know. And maybe it's something more than that. I won't give up thinking that it might be, and I won't give that up simply because the yearning itself is real and physical and oddly similar to the moment before orgasm, and it wants that same release into another place that lasts forever and ever amen, and I can hear the cynical voice inside myself say so that's all it is, the thing you always heard in those medieval mystic women's voices, the sound of sublimation. But it's that yearning that drives you through this life and wakes you up each morning expecting something, that says yes to this and that and again this. Here. Now. This life.

And so with Augustine. I expected lustful confessions and mystical revelation. And the thing that amazed me (yes, I am, in fact, amazed and stunned by this book; I've moved through my knee-jerk feminism and my postmodern cynicism as I read and have come out the other side stunned by his mind, which is to my mind as a cathedral is to my silly and pathetic dining room) is his dedication to his God, yes, of course, but also, oddly, to his vision. Augustine's vision is aesthetic (and I say that lightly; what do I mean by that, really?). Maybe simply that he's an artist, and his process is a writer's process, every sentence driven by the sense that this will save his life and maybe, God willing, mine. The stakes are high, there's urgency, and it is absolutely at every moment a sincere and self-conscious voice. His awareness of rhetoric at midpoint in fact is the rhetorician's consciousness of craft, of the way sounds manipulate perceived time, of the awareness of what you're doing as you're doing it (I'm saying this "because" and you know you're saying this "because") that we associate with post-Freudians, the thing we think in our sentimental postmodern funk has split us from our true selves, that we can reclaim only in some false Eden, some new age spiritual reclaimed childhood.

And there's his craftsmanlike awareness of how the mind works, the mind which is made in God's image and which is one of the gifts of the Holy Spirit. What I want to think about is Augustine's life as an artist, as a writer, of writing as a discipline.

He has a courageous and disciplined mind, not a superstitious one. It's courageous because he takes the gift of human reason, the thing that he's been given, and uses it as a lamp to illuminate dark places, and he's not afraid of what he'll find. He takes risks and chances. He goes alone. He's not afraid of heresy.

Why? Because underlying it all is an absolute faith in a universe that makes sense, and that's perhaps what faith is, finally. I know that it's the artist's faith. If this is religious faith as well, and I have no idea if this is true, then they're one and the same. The word "God" is a word. It's what that word signifies to you that matters. You can say "God" and think coffee cup or lamp or desk or chair, or you can say "God" and picture this faith. Though perhaps this is heresy itself. I'm speaking from a dark age out of little knowledge, though all of it is available to me, centuries and centuries of it.

I teach in a writing program. We like to think that these programs are very new and very American out of our own self-loathing combined with self-aggrandizement.

They aren't new at all. St. Augustine was a professor in an MFA program—a course of study known for centuries and centuries as the study of rhetoric. He was in all the plays as an undergraduate, and fancied himself an actor for a while. He was not unlike the talented guy you remember from your own undergraduate days, the handsome one who could act and write and sing, the one who made you swoon.

His studies came easily to him. His reputation grew. He had one post and then got another one at a more prestigious college. This was the fourth century. We'd barely begun to evolve, remember? Think how far you've evolved from your own parents, those well-meaning primates with the heartbreakingly unevolved hairstyles and tasteless kitchen appliances.

Women loved him, and he loved women. Who could blame them or him? His mind. The way he could talk. He took a lover. They had children together. It was eros that fueled his charisma, his writing and teaching, that kept him on fire.

He became a Manichaean, that medieval new age spirituality with its combination of Buddhism and Christianity and Zoroastrianism, its conflict between the spirit, which was good, and matter, which was evil, an irreconcilable duality. It helped him separate from his mother, who was Catholic. It was like piercing his tongue or becoming a Rastafarian. His conversion back to the Roman church and his rejection of Manichaeism, the reconnecting of matter and spirit, of good and evil, was also a return to the stance of the artist as opposed to the academic. Knowledge begins for the artist in the image, not the symbol. The language of the artist is metaphor. Things are both absolutely and clearly what they are—a comb, a brush, a tree, a rock, a cloud—and what they mean. Without matter, art becomes all air, meaningless abstractions, schizophrenic. Without spirit or thought, it becomes a chaotic jumble, without form. In the beginning was the Word, and the earth was dark and without form. Augustine meditates long and hard over Genesis, over the meaning of "the Word" and "form" as only an artist would, seeing God as a writer.

His conversion is in part an irrational and mystical one, but it is primarily a literary one. He read and thought and meditated and came to the rational decision that Catholicism contained more truth. This was a decision based on logic and study. (Why do I emphasize his reasonableness? I'm sure because my own experience with my mother's religiosity connected religion to the irrational, and finally to disintegration.) The conflict between his professional life and his internal life, between his stated and his acted-upon morality, becomes unbearable. He wants two things, and he wants them passionately. He loves his mistress. He has come to believe that it's a sin, and that he has free will. He's at the point where he can't live with the conflict any longer. It's midpoint. Something has to happen or his life will remain an inauthentic one.

"There arose a mighty storm," he writes, "bringing a mighty shower of tears. . . . solitude was suggested to me as fitter for the business of weeping," so he runs away from the friend who was consoling him so that "even his presence could not be a burden to me. . . . I cast myself down I know not how, under a certain fig tree, giving full vent to my tears; and the floods of mine eyes gushed out, an acceptable sacrifice to Thee."

And he "sent up these sorrowful words; How long? how long, 'tomorrow and tomorrow?' Why not now? why not is there this hour an end to my uncleanness?"

At the moment when the tension is released in tears, he hears a child's voice saying "Take up and read; Take up and read"—and this is the point at which I'm made the slightest bit uncomfortable, since I've watched in someone I love how easily the slightest sign can be interpreted, incorrectly, as the voice of God. He calms down, picks up the Bible, opens it up randomly, and reads the first place where his eyes fall, and it says "Not in rioting and drunkenness, not in chambering and wantonness, not in strife and envying: but put ye on the Lord Jesus Christ, and make not provision for the flesh."

And he doesn't read any further; "nor needed I," he writes, "for instantly at the end of this sentence, by a light as it were of serenity infused into my heart, all the darkness of doubt vanished away."

And he allows that insight to change his direction. And he wouldn't put it in these terms, but what he wants to do, clearly, is to write.

When he makes the decision to drop out of teaching rhetoric, which involved a lot of prestige and fame and some money (he was a proud man, and envious, and he was in the pipeline for promotions and even more fame and prestige and could have gone on that way but for the conversion), and when he gets the hysterical bronchitis that makes it difficult for him to teach even one more day, he says this: "But when the full wish for leisure, that I might see *how that Thou art the Lord,* arose, and was fixed in me; my God, Thou knowest, I began even to rejoice that I had this secondary, and that no feigned, excuse, which might something moderate the offense taken by those who for their sons' sake, wished me never to have the freedom of Thy sons. Full then of such joy, I endured till that interval of time were run; it may have been some twenty days, yet they were endured manfully; endured, for the covetousness which aforetime bore a part of this heavy business had left me, and I remained alone, and had been overwhelmed, had not patience taken its place."

And why is this not crazy? He thought about it, he has patience, he listens to both the passionate and the reasoned voice inside him, he keeps the connection between the inner voices and the outside world, and he builds bridges between them.

It would be so tempting, and so much easier, to give up thinking. But reason is the gift of the Holy Spirit, he said. And he presses on and he asks for courage, as a writer, when he's tempted to come to the easy epiphany, the line with resonance but no meaning, to drift into superstition. Later, when he wants to understand something and he finds himself faltering in front of the complexity of it, he writes "But what was the cause, O true-speaking Light?—unto Thee lift I up my heart, let it not teach me vanities, dispel its darkness; and tell me, I beseech Thee—the reason." And what follows will usually be an internal Platonic dialogue. Why this word? Why this? What does it mean? If this, then this? And how so? (And what drives me crazy, at this, my own pathetic and pale midpoint, is knowing that that dialogue is in part his own brilliant mind, but as filtered through the discipline of his education in rhetoric, something that had been discovered by human beings a millennium ago, and which can in fact be taught, but which was not taught in my own education in any fullness, and was not even hinted at in my children's education. This is, as I find myself repeating, a dark age.)

He moves back and forth easily between the concrete world and abstraction. "The body by its own weight strives toward its own place. Weight makes not downward only, but to his own place. Fire tends upward, a stone downward. They are urged by their own weight, they seek their own places. Oil poured below water is raised above the water; water poured upon oil, sinks below the oil. They are urged by their own weights to seek their own places. When out of their order, they are restless; restored to order, they are at rest. My weight is my love; thereby am I borne, whithersoever I am borne. We are inflamed by Thy Gift; we are kindled and are carried upwards; we glow inwardly, and go forwards. We ascend Thy ways that be in our heart, and sing a song of degrees; we glow inwardly with Thy fire, with Thy good fire, and we go; because we go upwards to the peace of Jerusalem. . . ."

The body is to a stone as fire is to the spirit. The Holy Spirit is to the earth as oil is to water. The part of us that is lifted by love, by truth, by the spirit—which are one—is understood in its process in the analogy of water and oil poured into a pitcher, with each substance mixing and naturally and easily finding its own place but remaining one.

He turns to contemplation and writing full-time. The religious life allows for that. There are contemplative orders. It required only that he give up his job and sex. The second was the toughest because sex was both, as I've said before, the fire that drove his work and the reward. He also knew that it took him from the writing. Time is precious. He took the risk that the fire would remain and smolder in sublimation. And sublimation there is in full in this text. And what happens? For the rest of his life he writes. He "pours out his soul in joy and praise." It's a soul and voice that still speaks with courage and wisdom across centuries and centuries of time. As close to an eternal voice as human beings can create, though he would argue with that. All his life he fought the internal battles. Lust and pride. He avoided those places where he knew they were searching for a bishop. When they heard him speak, they wanted him. Eventually, he became a reluctant bishop, and he had to remind himself of the necessity for humility. Teaching has its built-in pitfalls. He wrote first for his own understanding, and when he was satisfied or his search ended in praiseworthy mystery, he went on. "Whoso can, let him understand this; let him ask of Thee. Why should he trouble me, as if I could enlighten any man that cometh into this world?"

"I can't write! I can't write!" Kafka said, almost daily, in his diaries. And in the next breath went on writing.

So I've read two stories this week. The conflict between internal desires and the adapted life, the midpoint conflict, leads one man to canonization as a writer and a theologian, and the other to designing Lionel trains. They're oddly similar stories. Every way, says the Tao, is the same Way.

Marriage

And so, after writing for hours, my mind felt as shimmery as a metal plate or freshly minted money. I can see why writers work only a certain number of hours in a day. It's altitude training. The mind can engage with its own voice only so much before it stretches, thin and fine and brittle, and you need to turn your eye away from the rectangular space (screen or page) where it's been burning letters one by one by one, the inner dialogue branded onto this opaque gray that is in my case a ruled grid of dots, like cloud cover. I take the scattered particles that I've become and draw them back together—one by one. I brush my hair; I buy a slice of bread; I look out the window and watch a plane, and when the sun hits the center of the fuselage, I think that it looks like a pair of red-handled scissors flying. I want to follow that image, but I don't; I come back to—

The boys. Butler is in the NCAA tournament this year. The game's this afternoon, and so we talk about the game, our children, the weekend. I borrow a CD and walk to the Monon for some coffee. The bridge kids are out sitting a fine day—on the cement bridge over the canal, their hair dyed shades of purple, green, and red. The ducks' necks are also emeralds; there's new art glass in the art store window, red as berries.

And then? I meet my son at three to watch the game on a big-screen TV. My son! I say to everyone I see—look at him. He takes my breath away. I become foolish with pride. My son, see how he eats and walks, the yellow sweater and the white team hat. His heart rises and falls with the orange sphere as it makes its orbit (the basketball's color was invented here in the middle of the gray country). It orbits now from one side of the court to the other, day to night to day to night. And I've become an old woman and am glad of it. I follow the game with the same intensity as my son; I leap into the air with joy; we hide our faces in one another's shoulders; and the game, the community, our friends, my son, and at the end when our team loses, I watch again with pride as my son, momentarily wounded by the defeat, straightens himself, shrugs it off, and goes on.

And the point is? The point is that love and community draw you back into the world, and the joy wouldn't have been as great, or the sorrow—I wouldn't have felt it as deeply—if I hadn't spent the morning doing the other thing. I need both worlds so com-pletely that one is shadowed without the other. I've never medi-tated, but I think I understand from all I've read of it that art and meditation are one and the same thing.

There's an ecology of the imagination. In the hour between one world and the other, I wondered whether this whole thing—this project—wasn't crazy, and perhaps it is. And yet, the point is that I can leave it, and when I did and went outside the writing room, everything I saw was more alive, more precious to me. I wanted to taste all of it. Rather than being in conflict, the two worlds were tied together more completely after I'd worked. I've been a fool, most of my working life, to think otherwise.

The only danger, it seems to me now on this morning, the eleventh morning, was that for one half-hour, the transitioning, when I felt myself becoming shimmering particles that could disperse, I had to—by an act of will, or the grace, most likely, of other people and the world we've made—bring the particles back together into matter, this thing that loves her son and a silly game and sunlight and children and hates her dining room furniture and yet is blessed by all of it.

— — —

My daughter and her friends have been drawn into the drama of marriage. One friend's parents have separated this week be-cause the dad, according to my daughter, "likes this other girl and has for a long time," it seems.

The dad is boyish and charming—the key, a boy—he collects antique fishing gear and teaches tennis and sits around the family room with sports injuries drinking beer and leaving on fishing trips, but you can't help but weirdly forgive him, he's such a boy, so full of life. I'd like to be full of feminist outrage, but I can't be. The mother, too, also full of life, the one who has the party for the sixteen-year-olds the night the millennium turns and gives them beer but keeps their car keys and has them spend the night, earning all our gratitude. She's practical, a nurse, and so filled with energy and kindness. As the house is filled with creatures—sleeping children, children on roller blades, fish and guinea pigs named Mocha and Cappuccino, singing finches and green talking parrots with red and orange sunset-tinted beaks and a large dog and a cat named after a summer camp—a teeming life with bent-twig chairs and old paintings of the husband's wealthy, handsome, self-absorbed relatives. A large Catholic family, something Kennedy-like about them. Of course there's a girl, one of the husband's students.

In the middle of the week, my daughter is talking to her friend on the phone, and in the background her friend's beautiful mother is jumping up and down and screaming "Yes!" She's been out to dinner and a movie with her husband, and he's promised to stop seeing that other girl, my daughter says. My daughter thinks of it in terms of junior high school crushes and heartbreaks and her friend's upcoming birthday party, when they'd like to have the whole thing resolved one way or another. Though the daughter isn't sure she wants her daddy to come back. He's made the mother's life a living H-E-double-hockey-sticks, my daughter says. She's not mad at the dad, really—they went to a concert over the weekend—but she doesn't want to see her mother, to whom she has more loyalty, cry again.

My son says it's that midlife thing, and he gets this knowing smile when he talks about his own dad's constant cruising on the Internet for a red Ford Mustang convertible, just the right one, and I realize that from this point on—midpoint—my children are entering their mature years, their knowing, serious, adapting years—and everything we, their parents, do will make us seem to them, more and more, like children. Nothing in this world is more conservative than a teenager.

But about the family. The point is that it was and is a human system and has operated for years as this beautiful life-filled throbbing globe teeming with living beings, this fragile container. A human system of grace and harmony with its own life and well-loved individual members, but as in every human system there was a hairline crack, and it's along that crack that pressure is applied and the system breaks. And pain rushes in, and suffering, and it has become a wounded thing that they will choose to repair or not, and it will break apart and form new human systems, which will come, of course, with their own hairline cracks where evil will apply its pressure, because that's its function—to wound, to split—the catalyst—and the human being chooses whether to mend the thing, and either way we're reminded that no, we cannot create a heaven on this earth. "Perdition take my soul but I do love thee," Othello says of Desdemona, "and when I love thee not, chaos is come again."

And so it goes. We create things out of chaos. We hold them against chaos. Now and then chaos wins. The force of watery entropy is vast, and sometimes you want to drown in it.

When you write this much in one week, you question whether you've lost your mind. And I'll admit, I wonder. I guess the question becomes whether I can sustain it the six weeks by will, whether in the end these words connect at all to the world outside of itself. Madness never does.

If it's not madness, then I'm glad I chose to do this. It feels like choosing to run a marathon. And if I quit, what then? I won't believe in the possibility of my own freedom. No one asked me to do this, and no one would know if I stopped doing it.

Last night I dreamed that I told my friend things I had never told a soul, and she didn't judge me. This morning when I woke up, the first word that came into my head, whispering, was *atonement*. It's not a word I'd use or even understand or have even heard—at least not often—spoken. But perhaps that's what this is.

If you've read this far with me, you're watching me either going mad or becoming sane. Even I, the author of these words, don't know the ending of this one.

Every day I'll continue because I made a promise. To whom? To myself. A strange kind of fidelity. A marriage.

Last night, in the blue hour, I walked like a ghost to my dining room and looked out through the sapphire windows into dusk. The house was quiet. At the same time, the woman who lives in the house across the street came to her window and looked out. The blue deepened; her silhouette was as gray as the window shade against the evening blue. It was quiet, a kind of communion. The sun set, the light shifted; we turned back into our darkened rooms. The condensation of our breath on the glass between our houses.

It's Saturday. The morning I was looking for signs and reading Augustine, I decided to try opening the Bible at random, and I did. I realize these things are what psychologists call Barnum statements—one of the reasons the I Ching works, or the horoscope in the daily paper. Anything can apply to you if you're looking for a key, a sign to help you out of this miserable confusing freedom. The human mind works this way, wanting to put like with like. Artists count on it and scatter groups of images through the work like beads, hoping some reader will come along and string them. *Read this,* one friend of mine titled her book, *and tell me what it says.*

The heart knows what it wants, and it wants to have you listen and will read its desires into signs and portents.

The message wasn't clear. I didn't even finish reading it. I'm not entirely sure what it was it said.

One morning this week I talked to a friend on the phone and carried the conversation around inside of me like a flame inside the chest. Days later, the heart still burns, and underneath the skin, the kindling like the Holy Ghost, the thing you feel, the yearning, you carry it—the inner fire, the outer guide, the desti-nation—three separate things. The yearning is the same fire as this, and so. I understand the medieval sense that earthly impos-sible-to-sustain desire can be sustained at every moment in the reaching toward God. Without it you're as cold and dead as a stone, but I don't understand how it can be sustained for one moment without the body. Though if the conversation is long-distance, say, a memory only, entirely in the imagination, and it still causes this, then why couldn't you will another imagining, carry it with you always as though you were in love, because you know—you *know* that as soon as the imagined illusory beloved became a presence in your life it would start to fade. What if the yearning were in fact always sexual, the dragonfly mitered with another in flight, the shuddering of sea animals, the strangely erotic bodies of walruses and squid and bears, the swirls of accumulated time in wood, the climax that goes on and on and on in waves beneath the skin. How can they be separate from any-thing that's good—a catch in the breath—the fire you carry from the voice all day long underneath the skin even when you're apart?

Plague Sunday

Sunday morning. Raining and a chill in the air. The sound of sports TV rising up from the basement, the pout of women voice artists saying the lines of babies on the Rugrats cartoon from the family room. My son's at the gym, working out, and in an hour we'll all drive to Columbus to see my husband's shut-in parents, to get their groceries and medications. Sunday morning. A dark day today and yesterday as well.

In the paper this morning there was an article about the coming plague of gypsy moths. There was a photo of a tree covered with black caterpillars. They multiply so quickly they cover the ground, said a woman who spent last summer from morning until ten at night battling them. They infested the house; she heard them dropping from her ceiling. She carried an umbrella to the mailbox each day to get her mail. The stink of their dying drew flies by the thousands; you could hear their feces dropping on the ground like a constant driving rain. They eat the foliage off the trees, and when the leaves are gone from an entire forest, they spin a thin, fine web that carries them on to another.

I'd get rid of them if they came into my yard, my daughter says, and she can't imagine otherwise.

— — —

Last night I read Thomas Merton, and the gentle humility of that voice shamed me. Every sin, he says, comes from our wanting to be little gods. And C. S. Lewis, whom I read the night before, would of course agree. And then I see how this insistence on my own voice, my ambitions, is so much of what drives me. I-I-I-I-I.

I'm not obviously and outwardly ambitious. I've stayed in the same neighborhood where I grew up. It would have been smarter to move to New York, I'm sure. My students are often surprised to learn that I write books. They'll run across them unexpectedly. You're so humble, one will say, but I know at some level that's not true at all. I take this compulsion as mine, as something I do and that sends me soaring above the rest so far that I don't even mention it. I wait for someone to notice. It's the only thing, I'm sure, that keeps me from being nothing, which I will not stand to be. I worry about writing enough books that someone will remember me, that my grave will be on a tour of the cemetery. I. I. I. Though less so when I'm working than when I'm not. It's easier to ignore the twinges of jealousy, the anger I feel when someone makes a list and doesn't include me. Do you see how shallow I really am?

When I'm writing, I hope, it feels like joy and less ambition. I know the ambition sometimes colors the work itself. The self-consciousness. Do you hear the voice sometimes saying this is good? I come from the Midwest, where we don't shout, and in fact where when someone stands too tall, according to Homer Capehart, we cut him off at the knees.

Who's Homer Capehart? This guy from Indiana. We cut him off at the knees.

At any rate, I would like to write as simply and as unobtrusively as a Shaker designed furniture, and for the same reasons.

But there's that other thing.

I read Merton and was shamed by him and then went to sleep and dreamed. I'm sitting in the dark watching a movie with a friend, and some beloved presence comes in. It feels like something I've thirsted for, something easy and fine and deep. I touch his arm, and my friend leaves her seat so that he can sit next to me. In later dreams that night, the same presence comes into an anteroom of my office. Who is he? I don't know. It's night; he shuts the door and I kiss him, and in our joy we fill the room, the file cabinets and books, with pollen and with seeds. A muse dream. And when he leaves, I get on my hands and knees to clean it up, and the odd thing is that in the telling it doesn't sound pleasant, but in the dream every moment of it was fulfillment.

He's Catholic, and I can hear him saying that there's nothing in any of the commandments about not having sex with other women, only about not coveting another's wife or committing adultery; so whatever caused him to think he should get married? And once he did, twenty years later, at midpoint, why shouldn't he, a good Catholic, say that he can keep nine of ten commandments easily, and will? He believes in one God, he honors his parents, and on and on, and any argument, say, that he's putting another God before his God by breaking one commandment is nothing, he thinks, but sophistry. He'll have none of it. And if there's no prohibition against sleeping with women except that one commandment, and he keeps the rest of them, then what is it that's left of that commandment if you remove the sex from it? Well, he thinks, it's keeping promises and not lying. And lying to protect someone seems a forgivable sin if at some future time you atone for it. And as for promises? The day he promises never to break promises, he'll paint a rainbow on the roof of his house. Until then? What is it that causes this emptiness in the same place that days before was filled with joy? Who would have thought the children would take it as such a betrayal? It was so easy when you kept both worlds separate for so long. A little lie—what harm is it?

Monday

This is where it gets hard. Last week was a flying start. I have a great job, really, despite my complaints. Every year I have two spring breaks—the one from my own teaching job and the one I manage to take when my children are off school. During the first one I get caught up with grading, I do administrative work, I write, I shop for furniture. Last week was my first break, but today, Monday morning, school begins again. I've worked all day, and my daughter gets off the bus in an hour and a half, and I want to be home when she gets there. And between now and then I need to write today's entry and pick up papers from my office so I can grade them tonight; and my niece and nephew will be at our house all night while my brother and sister-in-law attend a banquet; and the sewer line has backed up into our basement, and all day long it's been raining.

I've spent the last two hours typing and revising the weekend's work, and in the time between taking my daughter to school and working on this book, I spent four hours on the Internet doing research for a book that's due at the publisher's April 1 if I want to get the rest of my advance.

I am more conscious than I've ever been of time. It's been years since I was bored. Time is the currency of my life. Each day I spend varying amounts on this and this and this. Both C. S. Lewis and Augustine spend pages defining time, and it's still a mystery to me. I follow the arguments while I'm reading them as I remember following Borges' argument, and Stephen Hawking's, but still, when I shut the book and begin my daily chores, I can't recall any of it. It's all so lovely but completely counterintuitive. I experience time as a metronome, and when it seems to go fast or slow, I never for one moment think the metronome itself has changed, and I can't really imagine it existing in any other way but forward. I can't see time going backward or its being circular or a dimension or anything but what it is to me, because if not that, then it's not time, and the philosophers and scientists need another name for whatever it is they're talking about. So there. I understand in the abstract that God's time is eternity, all present at each and every moment, but the thing about this life is how much I feel it nipping at my heels and pulling at my skirt, this annoying yapping dog, and the one thing I can never get my mind around, no matter how I try, is how time is a fourth dimension. I don't understand it any more than I understood algebra. Time is as real to me, as pressured and regular, as a heartbeat.

Last July my great-aunt died. I am, I realized as I sat with her, one-half the age she was on the day she took her last breath, exactly. We looked enough alike that we could be mother and daughter, or, even more odd, she could be me, at the moment when I'm ninety-eight, and I could be her when she was younger. We both taught at the same university. Her handwriting in the boxes of notebooks she kept throughout her life looks like my handwriting. The black-inked scribbling of quotations from everything she read in spiral notebooks, on note cards, if you were to shuffle our notebooks together, you wouldn't be able to tell which ones belonged to me and which ones to her. When she first moved into a nursing home, and I went through her things to sort them, this came as a deep shock to me. How did this get in here? My notes on Othello? How is this possible? I thought I was unique, but apparently the world has seen my kind before.

I was with her in the week before she died.

The Sunday before her death, I had one of those odd Sunday mornings when I wanted to go to church, and I drove to the church of my childhood and discovered I'd missed the service by an hour. I was dressed up, it was Sunday morning, I had this hour of unspent time, and I had remembered all week and with some guilt that it had been months since I'd visited her.

So I drove to the nursing home and sat with her. She was clearer than she had been for some time. Her memory was bad, and you could convince yourself that in your hurry to get to one place or another, your oh-so-filled-to-the-brim-with-obligations life, you had no time for her, and in fact she wouldn't remember if you were there. Some days, toward the end, she would sit in the hallway looking for her dead husband. He's looking for me, she would say. He's trying to find me, and I can't leave this spot until I see him.

On that day she was lucid. You know, she said, I want to find out what this means, all of it. This experiment. She gave me some wisdom that morning that gave me shivers. And now she's gone, and I can't for the life of me remember it, that wisdom. I wrote it down, but one week later my computer crashed, and I have no record of it anywhere. It now seems like a dream, one of those where you solve some problem and the next morning remember the feeling of having solved it but not the solution itself.

Those Things I Didn't Know about Death

That night, after I visited her and received her now-forgotten wisdom, she had a stroke. They called me from the nursing home and I went out, and for the rest of that week I sat with her.

There were things I didn't know about death. I didn't know that the legs get so cold, that death starts in the feet and moves its way toward the heart. When the nurses came in and felt her calves, they knew it was a matter of days until it was over. I didn't know that.

She had a "do not resuscitate" order, and it was my decision to honor it still. I didn't know that no matter what document you sign before this happens to you, in fact your will has nothing to do with the matter. It's a legal fiction, to protect the living. Once she's gone this far, her wishes count, but I could in fact have overruled them.

When Augustine's beloved mother dies just past midpoint, I was struck by how immediately he sees the departure of the soul and reflects it in his language. The "she" he refers to is his memory of her, her will as reflected in his memory of her actions and her voice and the still-living love he has for her, a love that has now joined that place inside the body where love gathers and presses against the throat, against the rib cage, the heart, all love, every kind of love. And after the moment she died, when he refers to the physical still-unburied presence of her, the matter of fact of her, it's as the corpse. It was so obvious a shift that it at first bothered me—not *corpse* but *mother,* something in me said—but no, upon reflection, corpse is right.

After each loved one's death, that place inside the living

person's body becomes fuller, more pressured, odd, like a balloon filling with more air, or water, and you worry that it's going to burst. It's like some particle of soul is released and begins to join with some particle of the living. It lives then joined to some other soul, in memory and in love, and is to the living in some ways fuller than it was in life, more real. And it grows and lives in some odd way as well. Every day my relationship with my mother changes, and with my great-aunt, and with my grandmothers. I think about them, I argue with them, and I slowly, slowly understand and forgive them and even more slowly understand that it wasn't they who needed to be forgiven but me. I was the one who should have understood while they were still alive, the one who should have asked for forgiveness but couldn't. And why? Because of that other pressure, the one of time, the sense that my time with them was somehow infinite and the things I had to do each day were more important and could barely be gotten done and would if it weren't for the demanding presence of their love. Mea culpa.

And so. I watched the body turn to a corpse, the soul still centered in the face, the hands, the beating heart, but the life gone from the extremities, which made very few demands. She could barely take in oxygen, and her upper lip was lax and blew out from her teeth with each breath like a curtain at an open window. That happens, too, the nurse said. I tried to talk to her as they say you should, telling her I was there, that it was OK to let go.

I wasn't good about visiting, but she was always happy to see me when I returned. She had no memory of when I'd been there last, and time for her had turned into something with very few markers, just the note on her bulletin board each morning telling her the month, the day, the season, and the year. She always remembered me, remembered where I worked, asked how I was doing. She would smile and say she had little to say, and I had no idea what to say to her, either. Talk about my job seemed shallow to me when she sat there all day in a wheelchair with this beatific smile. She said once that visitors were hard because they took her away from wherever it was she went inside herself.

I put a bird feeder outside her window and often forgot to fill it, though one of the nurses must have remembered, because it was almost always full. It's so interesting, she would say, all day long the way those birds go from the feeder to the tree and back again, always moving, and over there—she'd point to the gardener who now and then worked in the greenhouse across the way—someone will come out and put down a potted plant and then go back in and then later come back out and remove it. There's always, she pointed out to me, even in that square of window, movement. Something is always moving, and that interested her. And for that one moment when she pointed it out to me, I noticed that in fact nothing in the universe was static, and I could feel, for that one moment only, how deeply mysterious and beautiful that was and how I'd never noticed it. I remember that day asking her if the thing she was taken away from when someone came into her room and talked about trivial subjects was meditation, and she said that yes it was, and I now realize that she had become a holy woman. It was some kind of Midwestern Zen she lived in those last years. She would say the thing was to keep the emotions at an even keel, that people made them rise or fall, and her mind was focused on some dense floating place, perhaps eternity, perhaps outside the demands of daily time. She was a scientist and a deeply religious woman, and I know she understood what she was doing. This was her final challenge, and she met it magnificently. Did I say we were alike? In looks only, and in handwriting. I could never be that calm. And the thing about her in that last year was her response to other human beings. She had the most beautiful smile, lit with this internal light, and she would turn it out toward anyone who came down the hall. Her focus was always outward, and she made you feel as though you were an astonishing presence in the world. She did that with everyone.

The nurses would turn the televisions on in all the old women's rooms so that they could watch the soaps as they went from room to room, never an interruption in the narrative. My aunt would look at the television and remark on it. A biologist, she was always commenting on the obsession with romance—how odd, she would say—and once again, when I was in her room, it struck me as odd as well, like the constant movement outside her window, the pressure of mating and the way it calls so much around it into being, all of culture. I wondered how it would feel to be so completely above it, what you would turn your mind to, what would take the place of that desire. In her case it was a curious mind, this sense of watching a performance, some deeply intricate and mysterious pageant going on at all levels all around her.

That last morning I saw her conscious, she looked at the television for the first time with disgust—some kind of game show—and said, you know, there's so much more than this; I have so much more to offer still than this. And she told me the meaning of her life, and like a dream, I can't remember it. Mea culpa.

I have to go. Tonight I teach my seminar, and this afternoon I meet with students and answer email and messages. As the day goes on, the clouds and rain are supposed to lift. Tomorrow, if all goes well, I'll have more time for this.

Discipline

And all did not go particularly well. One evening class and one next-day meeting are enough to throw my concentration off completely. If I weren't committed to this process, I'm sure I wouldn't write a sentence today. It was the expanse of uncommitted time that allowed this to bubble up last week. It was like being in love. And this week, as the world intrudes again, it's a form that I hope will hold, like a rope bridge that I somehow want to believe is attached to something on the other side, something that's invisible but that I oddly still have faith in. It's like a marriage, and I've made a commitment to it. Wendell Berry talks about forms in his book *Standing by Words* and says that once you've chosen one, if you choose to leave it, you're standing in greater formlessness and chaos than you were standing in before you chose it. That was always difficult for me to get, how the chaos could be worse on the other side of the chosen form than it was at the beginning. It seems so unsymmetrical. But not if you draw it as a bridge.

If you were to draw it as a bridge, the form would be a solid metal one. On one side the bank is completely level with the bridge, the road from one to the other a smooth one; but when the bridge is abandoned, you fall into the gorge it crosses, and you have to climb back up somehow. I suppose this is why you cry at weddings. You could live your whole life meandering along the riverbank, but if you choose to cross the river, you're taking an enormous risk.

I'm thinking about marriage, of course, but what I'm really thinking about is writing. I've abandoned so many bridges and had to begin all over again because all these niggling things interfere too easily; it's too easy to get passionate about them. And once you leave the process, the entire bridge that you've been standing on—running, in fact, or even jumping up and down on—was, you realize, only in the spinning stages, nothing but spit and promises that disappear from underneath you and you can never recover it. The only thing that keeps a large imaginative project in the air is the power of its own projection, lift, and faith in the destination. Don't keep your promise to yourself, don't stick with the novel until it's finished, say, and whatever vision you had when you began is gone. And in the middle, when it seems as though you never had a vision, just holding on to the process keeps the entire thing from falling.

Meetings suck you dry.

I am, if all goes as lives are planned by retirement laws and pension funds, almost exactly at midpoint in my professional life. I've watched both women and men go through this point before me, and now I'm in it. When I was only approaching it and not in it, I had strong opinions about those going through it. Because I didn't know that they were going through it in the same way that I had no idea why you needed glasses after the age of forty. When my eyes started to harden and fog, I thought I was going weirdly blind.

And I thought all the women I worked with were going crazy and the men were withdrawing into senility. In both genders, the process was the same. Actually, it's just that the women were conciliatory and quiet up to the midpoint, then all of a sudden they lacked patience, would say what they thought in no uncertain terms, and the men, who up to that point had been assertive, would start sitting around the edge of the room at department meetings, would stop volunteering for things, wouldn't seem to care one way or the other about whether we required five papers or eight or twenty in freshman English. They wouldn't carry their weight, I thought, and the women were bitchy, and all of them seemed to be in some way withdrawing so that by the time they were in their mid-fifties you couldn't count on them for task forces or new initiatives, or if you could count on them it was only for the thing you counted on them for and not for one bit more. Where did they go? What happened to them? We've seen it all, we've tried it all. They saw it all, our endless meetings, as a spiral not going out and up toward some perfect form—the freshman English program that would save your life and would establish your place in the communion of the saints—but as a different kind of spiral, one circling in and in and in upon a muck-filled drain of wasted minutes, the undertaker's drain that takes the blood, every bit of life in you.

I spent the day getting to a meeting, being in the meeting, and getting away from the meeting. A wasted day.

I have a student who spent last year in Ghana. She's working on an honors thesis and is writing about African churches. Last night in class she told us stories, and we all could have listened to her for hours. She walked on rope bridges right underneath the canopy of a rain forest; she sat on a crocodile and ate some slippery yam concoction that slid down her throat without her swallowing. She watched souls possessed by spirits, a man turned into a snake and eating an egg from the ground in front of her. They thought I was an angel, she said, and we all thought that too—pale blonde and sweet, that kind of pale that seems trans-parent, as though she's emanating light. And the narrative she tells is the travel narrative, the same narrative someone traveling from Ghana to here and seeing us in that room would tell, that suddenly there were things in front of you you'd never seen— yams and amulets and rainforest canopies—and they remind you that the universe is so much richer than you thought, so much more mysterious and full than here where we are living. The traveler from Ghana would go back and talk about the orange moon through the casement window in the classroom where we were sitting, the opaque green slate that lined the walls, the sticks of cold white chalk, the swirls of inky time gleaming on the oak table, and the angelic voice telling stories about his own dull country.

— — —

All day Sunday it rained, and we didn't end up going to Columbus or to church, but I did go with my friend Barb to Industrial Goth Night at the Melody Inn near 38th and Illinois. I'm finishing up this other book, and I want to include an essay called "Industrial Goth Night at the Melody Inn." I have no idea what it will be about until I write it, which I need to begin doing.

The Melody Inn is right next to a costume store, and I think I pictured somehow the costumes come to life. I pictured odd people with white-painted faces and Elvira hair and vampire teeth. At some level I knew that Barb and I would be the freaks in this context, as in that Eudora Welty story where the women in the beauty parlor talk about a freak show while the permanent wave solution drips onto their necks and their hair is wired with metal/plastic rollers and the face powder settles into the damp folds of their skin.

It was an old bar, dark and moody. The windows were covered over with black plastic tarpaulins, and the mirror behind the bar was smudged with smoke and fingerprints. There was the obligatory pool table with the four obligatory boys who now and then lifted the table's edge and dropped it on the floor like thunder.

Barb and I sat near the back. The boys looked like any college boys. There were two tables with quiet heterosexual couples, the boys wearing black plastic Buddy Holly glasses like Mother Catherine's and the girls with short cropped hair and black t-shirts, one a little overweight. Not much there to remark on, finally. Nothing goth or particularly industrial.

At ten after nine a young woman breezes into the bar and collects the cover. The music starts, and the lights—primary crayon-colored lights on the tips of a bouquet of bendable black tubes—swirl and dip around the stage where the girl begins to dance. She wears a long black leather coat and under that a long-sleeved mini-dress, brown and painted with some black hieroglyphics resembling spider webs or skeletons, and the lights and another white light, a strobe, make her movements seem fragmented—which is the point, of course, because who wants a dance that's fluid motion and harmony in a world that is anything but harmonic? One thing is connected to the next by juxtaposition only, by proximity; the idea that there's some causal connection between one event and another is nonsense. It's chance; it's this and this and this and this and this.

Now and then the music sounds like factory noise. It's interesting to me that kids would connect the industrial and the gothic, since factories are the cathedrals of capitalism, the real cathedrals—more overwhelming than the malls, more awe-inspiring, less on a human scale. Here is a power larger than you are, more frightening.

We watch until we feel as though we get it. I'd love to be up there doing that, Barb says, and I agree. We could get up on the stage and dance; there's no one here but a bartender and two couples and four college kids playing pool and one industrial gothic dancer. We could let go, we could whirl and dance in our middle-class suburban costumes, but we won't. This bar is a rundown bar in a rundown white-flight neighborhood, and somehow this young girl had the courage to talk the owner into letting her do this on a Sunday night, and the entrepreneurial energy to advertise it in the Sunday paper, and then whatever it is it takes to dance like this all by herself on the stage with the sound man playing the discs and the light man starting the smoke machine and arranging the multicolored lights. And if we were to get up there with her and dance, we would look foolish, of course, but primarily we would be breaking an unspoken agreement we've made with our daughters—that this is their time to dance under the lights, that we never even want to, that we've taken the urge to dance like this and pushed it into the smallest space that it could occupy, and now and then it burns, and now and then we find ourselves choking on it, but mostly we know that it's a sacrifice, a stepping back, a winding tight of some cosmic spring for that humming jewel-like engine underneath our daughters' feet, the one with tiny metal teeth like a thumb piano that keeps them bobbing up and down so beautifully, and with such ecstasy.

I'm sitting in the drive-through line at Steak 'n' Shake as I write this entry, waiting for my order. The line is slow. It always is, which is why my family's sent me on this errand. They know I never mind waiting. I have a book with me in the car, and this notebook, and I feel as though I'm fulfilling the responsibility I have to feed my children (though, I know on this night, it's badly), and still I'm helping keep this imaginative thing, whatever it is, aloft. The only time I hate waiting in lines like these is when I haven't brought a book or pen.

☺ When I got home from work this evening, there was an email from Grace. She'd skipped the department meeting and had, I'd noticed, been skipping every one of them. Last year she had breast cancer and survived it. She hasn't been the same since, and the change is for the better. At one point when she was at her lowest, she said, she saw a bird that she associated with her dead father. And suddenly the entire world—the trees, her house, her body—turned into a single green shimmering light, the color of the world through a green glass bottle, and it was all one thing, and she felt her body as part of that thing, whatever it was. She's not a religious person, not the least bit mystical, and she hadn't asked for this.

And so. She promised herself that she would never waste

another day worrying. Her name is Grace. A mystical experience is true when it connects with the world outside of it and when the person who experienced it changes her life.

At any rate, she skipped the meeting and walked on the Monon Trail instead, and then she went into a cafe and sat on an old sofa drinking coffee and watching other people who had walked in off the trail. It was a great day, she said, and she plans on repeating it. If I ever want to head north on the Monon, she said, she'll be heading south, and I can meet her and we can go inside for coffee.

On Place and Time

What is it about Broad Ripple? I'm not there today because my daughter's home sick from school, so I'm working in my house and thinking about the place I would have been ordinarily. It's naturally on a human scale. There's that. The houses are small and ramshackle, bungalows that young married couples can afford to rent. And there's the mix of ages. Teenagers from the high school hanging out at the coffee shops and the Subway and the cyber cafe, and old women who have lived there all their lives. The Birkenstock store is sometimes closed for days because the middle-aged owners are doing something with their families or around their houses; and there are five or six vintage clothing shops run by younger men and women, and in the morning you see them bringing out the racks of coats from every decade of the last century. The couple who run Theo's Garden have planted the strip of green along the sidewalk with sunflowers, and on a warm morning he opens the door to the shop and there's that same green glass shimmer emanating from it that Grace described; and when all the doors are open to all the shops as they sometimes are, you get this feeling that each one is a window into another world, a world that's solid but that exists only because of all these human minds. How can I explain this? Let's say that the place itself is two-dimensional, a plane, and suddenly people weave these magical worlds that you can enter through these doors. In some of the shops there's a door at the front, and you walk through a human world like looking into a dollhouse or a Fabergé egg with an elaborately constructed scene, and then you can exit through the door on the other side and you're someplace else, some entrance to another place, and you've been changed by the place you've been.

I don't feel that way in a mall, which is cut off from any contact with the world outside of it, schizophrenic, but here, in this place, moving from one mom-and-pop place to another filled with freesia and art glass and lawnmower repair shops and old men making wooden cabinets in their garages and young people taking some old woman's 1940s wool spring coat and hanging it in a place of honor on the sidewalk, I feel what's good about human industry, the imaginative power of it. This, take this, make this and this. It's not a busy, crowded place like it would be in some other city. The sidewalks are easily navigable. You recognize faces. People are doing what they do. No one is wealthy here. And because it's on a human scale, you can live a human life. When you need a break, you walk out the front door and walk around the block or over to the trail, or you walk into one of these Fabergé eggs and marvel at the glass. You feel no compulsion to spend money. I still don't think I've gotten quite what it is I want to say here, how Theo's Garden is in fact a garden quite as amazing in its way as a forest. If I had made this whole creation, I think I would be so proud to look down and take up this place and look in its windows and think that the creatures I had made had made a place like this. I would think to myself that this is exactly what I wanted them to do.

And so, what's the difference between the place I'm writing about and the place where I'm sitting today doing writing? I live in a suburban island cut off on all four sides by highway. There are sidewalks, but if I went outside my door and walked, I wouldn't be able to go inside the places made with so much cost by each person's imagination. These are private places with no public space. When we need communion, we get into our cars and drive, and the only place there is to drive is a place made festive and communal by commerce, as it is in Broad Ripple. But what? What's the difference? I feel manipulated in a mall, deliberately cut off from the ground. I go from home, where I've been deluged with television and radio ads and catalogues arriving in the mail, to the place where I can buy those things, and then I go back home for more indoctrination. I've never seen one object in Broad Ripple, outside of the Starbucks and the McDonald's and the Subway, that I've ever seen an advertisement for.

We are in fact in a kind of maze surrounded by clear plastic walls that give an illusion of freedom. Maybe that's why I work on the inside of my house over and over and over again, why I so dislike my mother's furniture inside it. It has to be a comfortable cell.

— — —

Life is a tangled thing, and each day's challenge seems to be to loosen one knot of it. My knots are all internal, and I lack the proper skills, but still I pick and pull at them. Fifty IQ points, I was thinking last night, that's all I want, just fifty more. Is it too much to ask for? Oh hell, why not seventy-five. My stubbornness combined with seventy-five IQ points and I could get at those knots and really free them. As it is, my fingers feel all swollen and lumpy and the knots too tight, the thread too fine. Last night's knot was math-related.

It started when I went to pick my daughter up from school. Waiting in the car, I started reading a book on harmony. It's a book I picked up years ago when I was working on an essay about New Harmony, Indiana, and I thought it might be helpful. As it turned out, it wasn't, but since I'm working now on an essay about Industrial Goth Night, and in my research on the web I realized the industrial goth pages have links to links that go off in the area of surrealism and then John Cage and atonal music, I thought it might be interesting to think about what tonal music really is, and I remembered this book on my bottom shelf at work, and I brought it with me.

It's not a book, as it turns out, that I think I'll ever read.

Though there was a lot about it that was interesting. It was a treatise written during the Enlightenment, when writers were looking for eternal laws that implied benevolent design. The musician who wrote this book was a contemporary of Descartes. The music theorist who wrote the introduction started to explain Rameau's math, and suddenly, in a book that was supposed to explain to me why certain things sound good together and others don't, I was confronted with a page of algebra. I tried, honestly I did, to follow it. I was OK through the first equation, and then I got completely and absolutely lost. It made no sense to me at all.

And who should walk out the door of the middle school that very minute? This will seem hard to believe, but things like this happen when you live in the same place where you grew up.

I started laughing to myself when I saw him, and I had to look at him long and hard to convince myself that it was him. I waved at him, and he waved back. He hasn't changed at all as far as I can tell, though he was one of the young turks when I went to this middle school, and my daughter tells me he's one of the dinosaurs now. It was Mr. Dunham, my middle-school algebra teacher. I laughed when I saw him because I realized that I hadn't looked at an algebraic equation once since I sat in his classroom thirty years ago thinking to myself that I could never get this, and why should I? I couldn't picture myself ever needing it or ever once, when I got outside that classroom, looking at an equation again.

How could I have pictured myself thirty years older and sitting in a car outside this doorway waiting for my own daughter and looking at algebra voluntarily? And the memory and yesterday's knot made the whole thing into one knot with its own weird symmetry.

There are mathematicians whose life's work is to study knots, or so I'm told. I couldn't follow them beyond a handshake, and I'm the poorer for it.

Because I'm firmly convinced that much of what I want to

know I would understand with fifty more IQ points and Mr. Dunham's math class.

At any rate, when I turned the page away from the equations and there were drawings of strings and the way the strings are divided, which causes a doubling of vibrations, and the way there's some symmetry between the geometry of the string and perfect chords, then I understood part of what the equations had been trying to say to me, what Sally had been trying to say when she described *well-tempered.* I understood geometry when I got to it, but I couldn't even begin to touch algebra.

Though I wasn't quite interested enough to go any further.

So that night I switched to reading the *Times Book Review,* and there was a review of a new book that tries once again to define time. OK, I said to my son, help me with this.

The book was *The End of Time* by a man named Julian Barbour, and the reviewer was a philosopher of science from Oxford named Simon Saunders. To Einstein, he explains, time was "spatial." Like space, time "relates events to one another; it is an arena like space," Saunders writes. There isn't such a thing as past and future.

My son sprawled out on the couch beside me and read over my shoulder. OK, OK, he said. He wanted to be helpful. How do we know that it's really March 23, 2000? I mean, who invented clocks? There's not really such a thing as seven o'clock; it's all invented, right? I mean, he said, we've probably gained a lot of days and we don't know it. It could really be my birthday and I don't even know it.

It was extraordinarily sweet to me that he would think of that, would bring it back to his birthday. He's still such a little boy, though six feet tall.

OK, I said, but if, let's say, I decided to shave off my eyebrows right now, wouldn't there be the fact of this face of mine without eyebrows, and wouldn't I remember this morning when I had eyebrows? Nothing I could do would wish those eyebrows back until they grew.

My husband came into the room. He has the fifty IQ points I lack and takes them absolutely for granted. Life isn't fair. He sighs but tries to make it concrete for me. He draws an imaginary plane and situates my face with and without eyebrows and explains that it's maybe my mind wanting to draw connections that makes it all seem causal, like the explanation you give of a dream, the narrative you make out of separate details.

"But Barbour denies that time is like space," I read to them. "Events aren't situated in any fourth dimension and they are not related to one another by time. So time does not exist. But then how are we to think of change, of all the things we ordinarily think of as happening in time?"

"For Barbour," I read, "spatial things are the primary reality. We must begin in fact with shapes. Imagine collections of triangles, cubes, and other geometrical shapes. Think of an entire three-dimensional universe as built up of them and all their spatial relationships."

"So it's seven triangles past a cube," my son says.

And we go on through this article, sentence by sentence, through laws of gravity and motion, through superstrings and Newton and Einstein. Sentence through sentence I attempt to decode it, and my husband and my son attempt to help me. Why can't we feel it? I ask, and my husband says that it's because we're limited beings, and his easy, comfortable acceptance of that is why he's going back into the family room to watch the NCAA playoffs while I pick at these impossible knots.

And then we get to the interesting part. "Observe that neither Newton's theory nor Einstein's is what we use when it comes to our knowledge of the past. . . . With the exceptions of eclipses and the like, what we know of history comes almost entirely from records and memories. This, Barbour suggests, is the truer understanding of the past. Certain configurations contain within them copies of others; just as in a geologist's specimen there are shells, bones and spores, there is the past in petrified form. Each point . . . is unimaginably vast—a possible way in which all particles in the universe may be related to one another—and the history it encodes may be vast as well."

Some points are, Barbour explains, "time capsules." Most points in the universe perhaps are not. But our world is "highly structured, containing earth and living things, it is a time capsule par excellence. If this is how we really know about time in practice, perhaps that is all there is to it. There are only time capsules; you and I are in a single configuration, inside an instant. An instant is not in time, time is in the instant."

And in this particular instant inside an instant, Mr. Dunham is walking out the door of my middle school at the moment one of his former students is eternally not understanding algebra. And in the time capsule of my consciousness I remember him, and apparently he remembers me. And perhaps that's what we're here to do, to collect these observations and tie them together in narratives as real and essential to the universe as DNA and supernovas. And this maybe helps explain to me why I can sometimes see my mother's and my great-aunt's lives as a whole now that they're gone. Instead of being involved in the instant—my anger now, my love now, my sorrow now, my joy now—I feel as though I carry them both inside me as a memory, every instant of my life with them equal and without end.

In this time capsule of a family, my son took down a photograph of himself and his sister taken when he was six years old. I look just the same as I did then, he said to me, and then he laughed. Except, he said, that I didn't have eyebrows then and now I do. Which is true.

He thinks I'm funny, and he's right. Last night he stuck his head in the door and asked his father to get him up this morning at the usual time. And I fell for it, my husband said; I fell right into it. What time? he asked. The usual time, my son said again. You know, two cubes past a sphere.

Good night.

Synchronicity

On sphere day, yesterday, the day of strange synchronicity, I got a phone call from a friend who just returned from teaching in Alaska. It's like he was visiting the moon. They took me to a farm, he said, where the students are paid to research the mating habits of caribou. They paint the animals with these different colored phosphorescent geometric shapes and then watch them mate. Orange triangle mated green circle. Of course, I said, of course that's the way it was yesterday all day long.

My daughter's sick again today, so I'm staying home with her. She's lying in her bed across the room, asleep. I can hear her breathing, and when I don't hear her I watch the covers to see them moving. Her breath and mine, the breath of all the neighbors, and beyond that the breath of all the people in the cars and then the surrounding malls and offices and schools, this constant odd exchange of energy in the organic world. At one time the place where my house is was a dense hardwood forest. Between then and now it's been a farm. In our back yard we have a large oak and an elm and two ash trees and an expanse of grass, but we're in the middle of an extended drought, and if I close my eyes and only listen to my daughter's breathing and my own and the sound of the birds, I can almost feel the oxygen-rich moisture of that earlier air. Our brains are time capsules, and we fill them to the brim and what then? What's it for? They're time capsules that decay too easily even before the cylinder itself has been subsumed. Is that my husband walking down the hall? I've been here waiting for him, my great-aunt said long after her husband was gone. Though perhaps she did see him, moving down some hallway in some parallel world that only she could see.

I've been doing this now every day since Ash Wednesday, and I haven't told a soul. It seems immensely private, and I'm not sure why. I'm speaking in someone's ear, and I don't know whose.

Please forgive me as I take some time again to speak only to myself.

And so, what am I doing here? I feel as though I'm growing up. I've realized that all my own internal knots are formed when I'm not writing, that in fact they're internally written knots. I have this voice that constructs sentences and does that all day long whether I want it to or not, and that usually spends its time constructing unwritten sentences about office politics and dining room furniture and, even worse, ambition and pride and ego-driven hurts and on and on. And when I take that constant voice and make something with it, like this, it's as though I'm actually taking the threads and knotting them to some purpose and I move along some path. I've had the same amount of time I always have for the responsibilities of my life, and I'm doing them better, I think. I thought, when I began this, that my life was dull, but I'm more aware of little things and I find each day interesting, actually. I've wasted far less time wandering aimlessly in stores and much more of my time talking to friends. I've spent less money. I've been consciously thinking about things like how to budget my time and what's important. I find myself thinking about a Lutheran friend of mine who was taught that a human life goes like this: For twenty years you learn, for twenty years you earn, for twenty years you serve. I find myself thinking about things like humility and work, and I've thought a lot about Kant's idea of good will, and I realize as I'm writing this that I'm trying in some odd way to become more Christian, and I realize as I'm typing this that what that means to me has far more to do with actions than with any Midwestern fundamentalist idea of faith, which involves words, I've always thought, words that can't in any way signify the mystery that they attempt to signify. I don't want to sound pious (or unpious), but this is what I'm thinking about. I'm trying to be more present as I talk to people. Through this self-absorbed project, I've found myself, in my life outside of this, much less self-absorbed. I want to listen. I want to forget about myself. I find myself being less irritable. And I want to do this and can do it only because each day since Ash Wednesday I've tried to shape this time capsule. I'm not fighting what it is that I really want to do, and so I'm not resenting everything outside of it.

I've made some small changes. I go into my writing office every day I can. This morning I wrote an email to my department chair giving up the administrative part of my job. I direct a writers' series and have for fifteen years, and while it's been wonderful, I realized that the only reason I've kept that job is because I couldn't bear the thought of anyone else doing it, which has something to do with the ego strokes I get from it. How amazing that you thought of that, how incredible that you brought in that big an audience. I would rather teach an extra course and teach something that I want to learn myself.

Teaching, oddly, even though you're in a position of authority, reminds you to be humble. You can hear your own words tumbling back at you from a former student and realize that because you've taught her well, she thinks that she came to every one of her ideas on her own. And that, of course, reminds you that all those words you poured into her were in fact poured into you from some teacher you've long since forgotten. Oh, you haven't forgotten the teacher, but somewhere along the way you decided that the words sprang fully formed from your own heroic brain, and the less charismatic and quirky the teacher, the more smoothly the osmosis took place—the simple exchange of mind with mind, the imprinting of knowledge in another generation. There was a point at which, after graduating, I felt arrogantly superior to each one of my teachers. Though I was fond of them, I felt that knowledge was springing newly formed and whole out of my own clear wisdom, and during that period I felt condescending toward my education. It took me a year or two or three or four to realize how little I knew or would ever really know, how limited I would always be, and until just recently to realize how much I owed them.

The point is that administration isn't what feels right to me, and maybe it will turn out that teaching doesn't either. I hate the elitism and nihilism of academic life.

The important thing right now is that I have a sense of where this meditation is going. I've made some outward changes, and internally my life has changed in some profound way. I'm learning how to write an extended narrative, I think, the way that threads flow and ebb and then return. I'm anxious to write my next book, and I know what I want that book to be. This meditation is not religious in the sense in which I thought it might be. I'm not looking for some mystical pull toward some church or creed. But it feels religious nonetheless. I want to learn how to live each day with intense awareness. I want to learn what I can give back. I want to learn how to deserve the blessing of my daughter there on the other side of this room, asleep.

— — —

"As if you could kill time," Thoreau wrote, "without injuring eternity." For one moment this afternoon, sitting on the porch in the spring sun, I felt it. I knew what it meant, that word "eternity," how it's in a grain of sand, in fact, how you can taste it in the wind. I felt it, and there was no other word you could use for it.

This morning every tree in the world caught fire. First the magnolias, then the white flames of flowering pear, and then the fireworks of dogwood, and then the thick lush blossoms of the crab apple. In one day it happened, the sky an opaque Chinese enamel blue, and then like that, like sparks one after another. In the morning there were no trees blossoming, and by the afternoon they were everywhere.

I don't know that I can explain how gray this place is all winter. The Eskimos have hundreds of words for snow, or so we learn in college, and the thing that's missing here is a thousand words for gray. Dove gray, slate gray, cement gray, every possible shade of bluish gray and green gray and stone gray—granite gray and obsidian gray and limestone gray and quartz gray. There aren't enough English words for it. In the winter you become claustrophobic, the sky closing in on you. You want to scream or cry or punch a hole through the middle of it to escape. This is Prozac City, and there's a reason for that.

But this afternoon the sky has lifted, and the neighborhood girls are running through the shafts of knife-sharp light, and suddenly there's blue and yellow and flames of orange light between the slats of fence and purple lining the rooftops and sun so bright on the ivy it looks like mercury. There's a robin in among the purple hyacinths, and my husband has planted three new trees: a peach, a plum, a river birch. There's a crow on the finch feeder, his eye bright yellow and his head as blue as cobalt.

Midpoint

The doctor stuck a swab in the dark cave of my daughter's throat, and when he pulled it out it was covered with green pus and blood. She's pale and thin and her complexion is the color of dusk.

On the way home from the doctor's office we get ice cream, and the cold feels good to her. The penicillin comes in gelcaps. My grandmother used to pound round steak with a toothed hammer on days like this, pound flour into the steak and fry it crisp. My daughter's throat is swollen, flora-coated. The antibiotic works best when there's been at least two days of infection, the bacteria soaking into the pink flesh and leaving a space for this pill to begin its killing. God is in the lamb and the lion who eats her. It makes no sense to me. I only know that I would do anything in the world to protect this one lamb. Anything at all. I'd spit at God if he were in that lion. I'd grab the lamb and run and run to the edges of the universe and hide in the shadow behind some star. If this is the way the universe is made, I'd pray like hell to get outside of it. Who would I pray to?

The sun, the flowering trees, the smooth frozen taste of vanilla on the swollen throat.

— — —

Last night, Robby Strickland died.

Just last week he was playing basketball on our driveway. Mr. Neville, would you mind moving your car? Of course, of course. He'd play basketball until the lights came on.

It was nine o'clock at night, my daughter said. She heard it from her friends. He was on a go-kart up north of 91st Street on the Monon Trail, and he went off the road, down into the brush. There was a wire to keep people from walking into some field, some insane evil absurd horrible thin thin metal wire attached to two posts like railroad ties. During the day, you would have seen the wire. A simple reminder, a quiet reminder.

He was with two friends. My children have known all of them their entire lives. I want to make the connection between this household and his. I hate that I want to do this, but there it is. Robby played basketball in our driveway; we moved our cars for him He smoked cigarettes on the play fort behind our house. He walked back and forth through the yard beside ours. His older brother saved my son's life one summer when they were all playing in the drainage creek and there had been a storm and my son was almost swept into the viaduct. His family sold lemonade and cupcakes every year during the neighborhood garage sale, and my daughter bought a pair of his sister's jeans embroidered with the name they both share.

My daughter was home sick, so she didn't hear about it until her friends got on the Internet and began forwarding messages, great clots of messages forwarded and forwarded, gathering in waves of grief.

My son came in from school and said did you hear? Robby died. My daughter heard that one of her friends had been sent home from school because she was crying so hard the tears stuck in her throat. She had heard that the sister walked twenty blocks from our neighborhood to the place her brother died. I feel so sorry for his sister, she said. I kept imagining the mother, I said. It's funny, my daughter said, how we do that.

She hadn't heard the gruesome details.

The go-kart was stolen, my son said. The wire sliced Robby through the throat; it was cut back to the spinal cord. His friends saw it.

On the weekends the fathers work out in the yard. All day my husband worked on the pond and planted trees. One father jumped over the fence into our yard and talked to him.

At night the teenagers come outside the houses and walk. They're beautiful as deer. Three girls just went by our house, and I heard one of them scream. He's dead, he's dead, he's dead.

There are flowers in the yard outside his house.

I can't even begin to imagine how it feels to be inside there.

All day long the windows were open, and the sun was bright as hard candy, and the breeze blew the curtains in gusts like winding sheets. The day couldn't have been more beautiful, and we felt the clean air and the light and blue. It was a day it was almost impossible to swallow, as though something were closing up your throat and choking you. Beautiful and hammered fine like gold, that's what the day was like, and just as heartless.

What can you do? You feel it close around the neighborhood; you feel it. You hug your children every time they pass by you.

— — —

An hour ago I took my daughter to a friend's house. Whenever we're alone we talk about Robby. Her friend Jordan said you don't question fate, that the boy might have ended up someday in some far greater misery than this. It seemed to comfort her.

Jessie's mother Gina came out to the car and stood silhouetted against the night. She was the one who took Robby's sister to the school on Friday to clean out her brother's locker. It's what the girl wanted to do, and she wanted to go up to the trail and see where it had happened. There were flowers gathering, and someone had marked out a grave.

You had to think, Gina said, that it was Robby's time to go. The wire wouldn't have harmed you if you'd been on a bicycle or walking. It was there to keep cars from going down in the gully. Someone had put it there for safety.

The wire was at the height of Robby's throat as he rode on the low machine. If he'd been on a bicycle or walking, it would have cut him at the knees, tripped him, caused him to flip over. It was the time of night, she said, when the wire was the exact slate color of the sky. All day long it had been visible, and only at this hour of the night did it fade into the background. Dusk. A few minutes later and it might have flared sunset colors. It was only eight feet wide, the width of the road there, set up just for Robby on the night he would ride a go-kart in springtime adolescent joy off the side of the path. The wire was at the height of Robby's throat. His two friends were there with him. They'd stolen the go-kart. They'd painted it a different color so it couldn't be recognized.

At the high school, she said, they had counselors waiting when the kids walked in. The counselors let the teenagers walk up north to the trail. At the middle school, there were kids walking down the hall crying. I saw this girl wanting to go up to the sister, Gina said. She walked up and walked away and then went up to her again.

I went over to her and said you know it's OK, you can hug her. I didn't know the brother, the girl said, and Gina said at a time like this we're all brought together. It affects all of us.

Dusk: Third Sunday in Lent

Gina's face was dark with extraordinary beauty and with sadness. It made me start to cry for the third or fourth time that day, and my daughter was embarrassed. I don't know that Gina knew. It was dusk, and I turned my eyes away from her face.

The neighbors' flag was backlit with the light of the family's windows. The television flickered inside the house like flames.

The flag was a vivid wounded red, transparent as a leaf, a child's fist cradling a flashlight in the dark, the blood seeping through the fingers.

I turned back to Gina's face. All around her, the night had turned the silver gray of razors, knives, and wires. Not a one of us moved. How could we? They could be anywhere at all. Put out your hand and feel the sharp edges, camouflaged in the pearl gray of doves. Razors, knives, and wires. The soft, sweet, deceptive night was filled with them.

Oh that I knew where I might find him! that I might come even to his seat! I would order my cause before him, and fill my mouth with arguments. I would know the words which he would answer me and understand what he would say unto me.

On Fragility

A writer's confession: I am ashamed of my self-absorption. I am ashamed of the way that, when things happen, I'm eager to observe and use them. I'm ashamed of the way that makes me get this odd joy out of tragedies. I'm ashamed of being at times an ambulance chaser. When there's a fire in the neighborhood, or a murder, I'm the one who talks about and contemplates it long past reason. I'm ashamed of how it takes me outside myself, and how I long for that. I'm ashamed at some level that when I found out about Robby's death, there's a part of me that thanked God it wasn't one of my own family. As though tragedies like these are sacrifices the community makes, like a child going down the mouth of a volcano. It's Passover. I'm ashamed of that and ashamed of this confession.

— — —

There were hundreds at the funeral, all ages, and everywhere you looked there were weeping teenage girls and teenage boys with their heads bowed, trying not to weep.

John Murphy's mother came up to me and hugged me, because every mother I saw there felt bonded to every other one and every one of us was crying.

We moved slowly into the sanctuary. It was a Catholic church, a light-filled modern church with white walls and a risen Christ rather than a martyred one, and stained-glass windows high up near the ceiling. Christ's robe was a fiery reddish orange, the color of a burning log, and the red fell on all the women's hair.

The family chose Ecclesiastes for the text—to everything there is a season, and in Robby's season, the priest said, it was his time to dance. In his homily the priest spoke of Robby's having gifted all of us with his presence for fifteen years, that it was God coming through Robby's smile telling us to lighten up, to enjoy this world.

Last night my daughter was talking about Robby's smile, the thing you most remember about him. Her friend Jordan had gone to the calling at the funeral home, she said, and when the sister saw her brother, she ran out of the room screaming that they hadn't made him look like he was supposed to look. It wasn't my brother, the sister cried. What have they done with him?

He was wearing a turtleneck, my daughter said, which he never wore, to cover the cut in the throat, and you could still see places underneath the makeup where his face was bruised. Robby would never dress like that, would never have his hair like that, and it wasn't his smile.

You know how Robby was always smiling? my daughter said. They tried to make him look like that because that's what everyone told the funeral director about him, but it didn't look like him.

Why not? my daughter asked. You just pull the corner of the mouth like this, she said, and she tried to mold her own face like it was Play-Doh.

Of course it didn't work. My smile is big, too, she said. When she pulled the muscles up by hand, she looked like a clown. Or a doll. You can paint a smile on a doll's face, I said, but it doesn't look any more natural. It's not the muscles in the face that make your smile, I said. It's something else.

It's like they can't get the skin right in video games? she asked. Maybe like that, I said.

— — —

The priest said that Robby was full of life, though not always the life his parents would have had him live. And his vision of Robby and this soothing ritual was like theater, the way it allows you to face the most imaginable terror and gives it context and meaning in a community, only in a community.

And then there was singing and the priest holding the Bible up in the three directions and walking around the casket with incense, and there was the communion. It was a good mass. His brothers and sisters followed the casket out of the sanctuary, and then there was his mother, ashen as death, leaning against the father; she could barely move, and I could feel the woman beside me start to sob, and all the other mothers and the fathers.

Several hundred of us there, and all of us connected through the schools, the churches, and our children. How could you live in this world otherwise? The horror of it faded; we focused on the life that Robby had lived, on protecting all these crazy children who were left.

During the service, two or three of them snuck outside to smoke, and afterward there was a car full of teenagers, the girls crying, the boy driving with the bass on his radio turned up so loud the ground shook. *Please keep them safe.*

— — —

In this morning's paper:

By Matt Grenson, AP

When the Relativist Heavy Iron Collider begins operating in May, it will recreate conditions that have not existed since the dawn of the universe. Could that mean the end of the world?

Last year a British newspaper charged that the new physics experiment on Long Island might somehow generate a black hole that would swallow the plant or perhaps turn all of creation into some kind of deadly "strange matter."

Given that the collider will hurl particles into one another almost at the speed of light, generating temperatures of a trillion degrees and creating a substance that has not existed for 13 billion years, it is easy to imagine that it might cause some kind of catastrophe.

But a panel of physicists commissioned by the Brookhaven National Laboratory said after the article came out in *The Sunday Times of London* that every imaginable disaster scenario would be impossible—or at least unlikely.

The black hole idea was easy to dismiss. Although the RHIC collisions will pack an awful lot of energy into a very small space, their total impact is roughly equivalent to a mosquito hitting a screen door. Hardly enough to make a black hole.

Another scenario was at least theoretically possible. Maybe a collision could create strangelets, a new form of matter that would also transform everything in contact with it—at the speed of light.

"This one you can't absolutely say no to," said Brookhaven physicist Tim Hallman. . . .

There's one more disaster scenario. Somehow the massive energy released at RHIC could jar the universe into a lower vacuum energy state.

The vacuum state is sort of the energy level of empty space. It is possible, but unlikely, that the universe is not in the lowest possible vacuum energy state and that RHIC could jostle it to a less energetic level.

"This would trigger a chain reaction which would literally swallow up the whole universe at the speed of light," said Brookhaven physicist Tom Ludlam. . . .

Physicists say the collider will begin operating some time in May, depending on how long it takes to power up the superconducting magnets and fill the machine with gold nuclei. It typically takes months to get a high-energy particle collider going.

— — —

The teenage boys drove out of the church parking lot in their cars. It was, despite the funeral, time off from school, a bit of a holiday. Their blue shirts and their fresh crisp white ones and the yellow shirts and the miles and miles of khaki for their pants and their hair combed and gelled and their girlfriends with black pants and dresses. The life inside of them. They will grow up and go to college; they will have a senior prom; they will get their class rings engraved with their initials, with a stone commemorating the special day of their one and only birth; and they will grow up to be mothers and fathers and lovers, to be accountants and scientists and teachers.(And some of them will drive their go-karts or their particle colliders or their cars or their bicycles or their backhoes or their baby carriages or their marriages or their careers off the road, down into the dusky places where wires have turned invisible in the dark.)

Postscript

I went to get my hair cut this afternoon and said to Cidy, the woman who cuts my hair, did you know that boy who was killed on the Monon Trail? I told her I'd just been to the funeral. She said that she'd been walking up where the accident happened over the weekend, and she saw flowers there and teenagers standing there and crying. Now and then she stopped and spoke Spanish to a woman who was sorting through magazines on the table in her waiting room. The language was soothing and sweet to me. I had no idea what she was saying; it was just the music of it, the lilt of the human voice singing over day-to-day things, those magazines, the windows that need cleaning, the brilliant sun.

At night, Cidy said when she turned back to me, the trail is the darkest place in the city. I've been up there with friends in the middle of the summer, after nine o'clock, and all you can see are fireflies and now and then a light from someone's house. If I were a teenager and I had a go-kart, that's exactly where I'd want to go—that paved straight road, with no cars and no lights so no one can see you.

And the odd thing, we agreed, is how magical the trail is

during the daytime, how it draws everyone in the neighborhood to it on the finest days. There's something spiritual about it almost, she said. How could anything like this happen there.

She didn't know the boy, but she knew me and she knew the woman I was sitting next to at the funeral, and she knew the woman's daughter and she knew the woman's sister and her sister-in-law, and she knew we were leaving for spring break this weekend and she wished us well. Her silver blades had snipped through all our hair, that thing that keeps growing after death, they say, and we were all here in this one place at this one particular time in the history of this place, and our lives were a sweet and fragile sorrow bound together by some force we were more times than not completely unaware of. Today you could feel it in the air.

Children

I've lost track of the numbers of the days. Each day just is, and this is a new one.

I've been trying to make it a point to talk to neighbors when we find ourselves outside. It's difficult, because of the way the neighborhood was built, for suburban privacy. There's just enough distance between the houses that it's difficult to say hello without shouting, and so you and the neighbor have to be at the mailboxes at the same time or you both have to be in the mood for talking and begin your slow moseying toward one another. There's something in all of us that backs away from that. There's not enough connection that we don't have to begin again, each time, with small talk, and it's wearing. The small talk can't involve our jobs because we'd have to explain too much. And we don't gossip, so there's not much left to bind us together. We talk about sewer lines and landscaping and how the roof is constructed and whether we're planning on moving or building an addition.

Except when there's a tragedy, and then you realize how much the real structure of our lives is this community, how everything else disappears like the holes in a coral reef, and you're left with this and you see that it's what's keeping you grounded in the real. So one of my goals is to talk more to my neighbors, to really talk to them.

And so. My daughter had more stories about Robby's calling. Many of her friends went, she said, and everyone put something in his casket. Flowers, of course, but he'd just started working as a bagger at the Marsh grocery, and they buried him with his Marsh pin on his jacket and his employee ID in his hand. Of all the things she's told me, that detail is the one that most completely breaks my heart.

Robby was a twin, and his twin sister, the one who ran from the viewing screaming, went home and got Robby's hairspray and his gel. The undertaker had fixed his hair in a way that Robby himself never would have fixed it. So she combed his hair with the gel and sprayed it for eternity and put the bottles in the casket with him.

Girls took their earrings and pinned them to his shirt. They had dressed him in his new spring break clothes, his khaki pants and flowered shirt over the turtleneck.

Oh lamb of God who takes away the sins of the world, have mercy on all of us. How can my daughter hear these stories, and tell them, without breaking. A hollow space and nothing rushing in to fill it. Such fragility.

Wednesday

It's been almost impossible today to work this in. In forty minutes my daughter gets off the bus, and I've spent the entire day working. There's a big event tonight at Clowes Hall that I'm in charge of, and all day long there have been fires to put out. Douglas Adams's plane will be an hour late, and we had to find a wheelchair to get Ray Bradbury from the hotel to the hall, and every addition or change involves a series of other changes, and I'm the air traffic controller in the midst of them. The phone is blinking its digital numbers at me, asking me to check the messages, and I need to write my introductions. But I'm going to carve this forty minutes of time out for this.

I was thinking about Adams and Bradbury, and how both of them create metaphors, as all artists do, but how they both have taken metaphors and constructed them into things that you can physically touch or literally see—video games and, in Bradbury's case, buildings. Space Ship Earth at Epcot Center is his design, or rather, the metaphors are his, and someone built them, poured a building around them. And I was thinking how, when you walk through the metaphors of that building or one of Douglas's games, or through a book or painting or dance, it's like you're walking through a space constructed not to be simply what it is but what it is and also what it *means*. And I was thinking that if human beings are in fact created in God's image, then what we mean by that might be that we are capable of creating environments that have both beauty and meaning, and how easy it is for other human beings to sense the meaning, and how natural, even if you can't quite put it into words, and how frustrating it is when someone looks at something you've created and sees only chaos. And how much of that meaning is not particularly conscious in human beings, or chosen, how it seems to grow through doing the thing itself, and through attentiveness and how what we are attentive to may be the meaning that is there. That perhaps we're walking every day through a created thing, a structure, that the things we do each day, the movements we make, are through something very much like Space Ship Earth, something with a path, with doors and tunnels and unexpected lights, so that it feels sometimes as though you're standing in the dark with nothing holding you, but in fact you're not.(If there is a God, how frustrating it must be to think that you created this structure that is in itself a kind of metaphor and built it with sentient beings who might be able to feel, because they have a sense of metaphor, its meaning, and to see them walk right through it uncomprehending.)

So what is that yellow gleam in the concave disc of the doorknob on the six-paneled door across the room from me? It would be tempting to see the cross and think that meant something. Perhaps it does, but of course everything I'm looking at inside this house is an Epcot Center, an environment constructed by human beings. Human beings are part of the design, the hardwiring of our brains, and what does that mean, and how does this hardwiring fit within the world I see if I turn away from the inside of this house and look out the window at the same yellow gleam in the forsythia in my neighbor's yard? The yellow of the brass, the bush, the bird's eye in the feeder, the yellow of the bus full of schoolchildren that just appeared on the street behind me. Draw a line between them and you have a structure, and the metaphor behind this particular structure is what? Joy, perhaps. Praise. Blooming. My brain is structured to make those connections and be pleased by them. Doors opening onto something I can't quite name.

My daughter's home from school.

On the Cusp between
Wednesday and Thursday
11:30–12:30—Waiting to
Fall Asleep

Just home from the lecture. Sometimes I hate my job, and then there's an evening like this that feels like church should feel but never does.

Bradbury went out on the stage in his wheelchair. It's late, I'm tired; I can't really explain how amazing it was.

When he talked to Adams before the reading, he told him that he shouldn't simply read, that that would bore the audience, that he should talk about his life. When I asked Bradbury who should go first, he said that Adams should, because, he said, "I'm good. No one can really follow me."

Oh dear, I thought. Bradbury's such a sweet man, but eighty years old, and he's had a stroke; and when we picked him up the night before, he had to stick his feet out in front of him because the wheelchair didn't have a place for them. He seemed so fragile in his blue suit with his feet in hospital slippers held up in the air and his cane clutched to his chest, and his one simple canvas bag with notes for his lecture and no luggage. He would sleep, obviously, in his underwear and get up and put on the same suit. And when he said that about how he would give his talk and get the ovation and then leave, I thought to myself that he was old, and I found myself touching him on the shoulder and speaking louder than I should, as though he were deaf. It would, I thought, be sweet and an event, but he would ramble and weave, and the talk itself wouldn't be memorable.

Adams came on, and he was a showman. He read pieces from *The Hitchhiker's Trilogy*, and they were funny. He walked back and forth across the stage and the audience laughed, and I thought about this poor old man sitting in front of a monitor backstage, watching. "He's good," Bradbury said when Adams was done; "he did absolutely the right things," and I thought yes he did. How could Bradbury be better than this? Adams was an actor.

And then Bradbury came on and started to tell his story. My story, he said, and he proceeded. I did this and this and this and this. And at some point you realized you wanted to listen to him forever. Why did his stories about himself seem so oddly selfless? In part it's because you realized that his life was a gift, as the minister had said about Robby, and that he wouldn't devalue this one gift, the one he was, any more than he would devalue someone else. I did this and this and this, and the point behind him, the thing he came back to, was this is what I've learned and you could do this too, and this is what I wish for you. He wrote *Fahrenheit 451* in nine days out of simple passion and joy. The job of teachers, he said, is to point the way to the library. It's all there, he said, every bit of it. And so he started working in the library, paying ten cents an hour to use the typewriters. And at some point he became oddly passionate about dinosaurs, and he read everything about them he could find, and what? He wrote a story and it got the attention of John Huston, who asked him to write the script for *Moby Dick,* and he stayed up for nights to do that until he said "I am Melville" and he wrote the script. "Why did you ask me to do it?" he asked John Huston, who said that it was the mournful sound of the whale in the story about dinosaurs. Selling the script meant Bradbury had money to travel just a few days beyond when he had cried one night because he thought he never could afford it.

And the point is that he followed where passion led him, and the dinosaur, which seemed like an exit ramp on some unfinished interstate, became a connecting bridge between one life and another because he let it.

And you want to know why we're here? he asked, and he said that he would tell us. You've thought of this yourself before, he said. The universe is eternal, he said, and it continues so deep on every side and with such beauty, it's astounding. And why would you create this much beauty if you didn't intend it to be seen? We're the ones who hear the tree fall. We're here as witnesses. We're here to see the universe, to respond to its mystery and power. Who else would do it? Someday, he said, there won't be human beings on this earth. Maybe ten million years, maybe twenty. We'll have to leave this place. And when we do, we'll take murder and violence with us, sure, but we'll also take Shakespeare and Emily Dickinson.

You have a short period of time, he said, to witness the miracle of this universe. Why should it exist at all, and why should you? And if you miss the chance to witness, he said, you'll never get another chance. This is it, your one and only life. Our purpose is to celebrate that mystery.

So it's midnight now, the beginning of another day. Goodbye to the person I used to be, goodbye. Hello to this new one. I think about that fable that says there are twelve righteous people who hold up the world. If that fable is true, I've been privileged to meet one of them.

A Window into Radiance

Sometimes you listen to writers talk and you leave feeling as though you're living in the darkest times, and then you listen to other writers talk and you feel as though the times you live in are extraordinary.

Since I was in college, the thing I've loved about universities is those days, almost like holidays, when some great mind comes and everyone sits around to listen, and you leave seeing the world outside the listening space transformed by what you've heard. In college I spent several days listening to Buckminster Fuller and another several days listening to Alan Watts. I didn't understand half of what they said, I remember, though that made it almost better, like I was listening in to some mystery being conveyed to me in Latin. And I listened to John Cage in the same way; I still have so much of his book *Silences* memorized that I'm afraid at times I borrow from it without knowing. Good music, I remember him saying, is like a good life—the proper mix of freedom and restraint.

And yesterday I listened with my students to Douglas Adams answer questions and then, once again, Ray Bradbury. Adams was wonderful, very smart, and his vision of this time was an exciting one. This is, I know, the beginning of a new-century euphoria, and anyone who might find this document in an archives of strange diaries by women written at the beginning of the twenty-first century, and knowing whatever dreadful things are bound to occur in the next hundred years, will point to it as naive. When the century turned three months ago, I remember sitting in the Monon Coffee Shop with Marianne, a poet, who said how oddly celebratory it all seemed, how the new century really did feel like something new, a different kind of air, a fresh start.

Adams's excitement centers around the Internet, which heals, he says, a sense of alienation we've had. *Interactivity* is the big word now, he says. We didn't need a word for that before, he said, because everything in our environment was interactive and social. And then it got so it wasn't, and so now we need a word for its restoration in the same way that we don't need, right now, a word for people with only one head, but we might need a word for it at some point in the future.

Sometimes I feel, he said, as though we've been engaged in a great experiment to turn matter smart. When this world began, there were more dumb things in it, rocks and things, and then you'd look around and there was a little bit of celery or sponge. And we've taken buckets of sand and made them into silicone chips, and now we're putting those chips into other things and making more things smart.

And then Adams left and Bradbury came in, and once again the students were spellbound. It wasn't so much what he said, but something about his spirit. I don't get it, one of my colleagues said, what there is about Bradbury, and I say it has something to do with enchantment. If you didn't get it at a certain age, then maybe it's too late for you.

One of my students had a better answer. He said he'd seen one or two great human beings in his life that seem to radiate some divine love, and that was true of Bradbury. You could see how a simple human life could be magnified in myth if someone had that radiance, and how that radiance has to be used for good, and what separates a great teacher from a despot.

He was so beautiful with the children who came up to him. If some spirits seem like lenses into darkness, his presence was like a window opening into radiance. An icon. You could see through him into mystery and light.

BOOK TWO: CAPTIVA

Saturday—

Five hundred people on the plane, one used to transport soldiers, and it slides down out of the gray clouds into air the color of butter.

The colors! my daughter says. I had no idea there were colors like this, she says—lush green and red hibiscus, purple azalea, and the jewel-toned water—emerald, sapphire, fire opal. Why would anyone live in Indiana? my son asks, and I say because of the colors.

When we used to travel to my mother's house, the year we lived in Florida, I was amazed by the subtle shades of gray and blue, and all the vivid colors seemed, by contrast, gaudy. Though you can't see one palette, really see it, without the contrast to the other. Interesting that *palette* also means to taste.

We spend the afternoon at the beach. A little boy waddling in a lime green suit, and all the children in a triangle of silver glitter in the surf. My children's bodies emerging from the olive ocean, stars gleaming all around them, fish scales.

It's night now. The air is the temperature of warm milk. It smells like damp paper, an old attic; there's a bottle-green glow from a shaded lamp in the boat across the harbor.

Today I saw white egrets and manatee. Every light is a candle in the water. There are teenagers roaming in the dark, and I'm waiting up for one of them.

I hear his key in the lock.

Sunday—

Twelve white plastic chairs and palm trees facing the water. A mangrove forest filled with white birds. The swimming pools are rectangles of aquamarine ether. I've eaten too much. The insects sound like squeaking tennis shoes. Down the street, there's a restaurant draped with bubbling Christmas light. Out in the blue-green ocean the fish make the same bubbles with their gills. Egrets stalk lizards on their black stick legs.

What do you do in paradise? You eat. You float on water. You eat again. You realize that you'll live another year for just this taste of it.

Do people actually live here? Boats come in and out of the harbor. There are people who work here. They make your meals and braid your hair. They drive the trolleys and stock the shops with earrings made of shells. They walk up and down the beach at night with metal detectors, looking for discarded watches and old money. They make your bed. They drive out every morning from the mainland.

Monday—

What did I expect? On vacation now and then, the narrating voice will play inside one's head, but it says things like "I like red-orange at this particular latitude but not at home," and "I like bright yellow and teal," and "The ocean is the color of a pop bottle." And that grass looks more real than that grass over there, and why do palm trees lean so chaotically, as though they haven't been blown by the same wind?

I think about how the wind and surf drown out human voices except for the ones right next to you—your children and your husband. At the beach, you huddle in a shell of sound. You laugh and whisper, rub oil on one another's backs; you take photo-graphs—slick color representations of stillness, like a paint chip where the color is saturated clear through, a rubbing from a gravestone. You'll look at those pictures years from now and say how beautiful we were, how happy we were together, this family.

This afternoon I followed my son over to the beach to watch him in the surf, as though I could do anything to save him if he started to drown, as though he still needed me for that. Over six feet tall, he starts playing football with other young men, and there I am huddled underneath a yellow umbrella wearing an absurd khaki hat, a towel over my feet, a yellow-orange swimsuit cover-up—a small woman still watching her son with the same intensity I watched with just yesterday when he was an infant. Superfluous now in this situation, unnecessary, just now realizing and being proud of that. Anyone looking at us would have no idea I was sitting there all maternal as a bird watching a nest of eggs, still ready to risk my life for him.

How did the time go so fast? I've taken this week off from teaching other people's grown children because in two more years this one will be gone to college as well, and I'll want these memories. It was only a day or two ago, it seems, when he was born, and I had this sense that my whole life was consumed with being a mother, that I would never write another word. But I did write, and it was the children who tied me to the world I needed desperately to see.

Tuesday—

A squall blew in from the ocean today, and it was one of those vacation days spent with squabbling children.

At night we took a boat ride, and they'd hired a Jimmy Buffett soundalike songwriter to sing for the hour. Every night he sings as the boat draws a line around the island. One island over is the place that inspired Jimmy Buffett to write "Cheeseburger in Paradise." Why isn't this man, the soundalike, with all the same material, the famous one? He asks himself that question sometimes at night. Is it, he thinks, because my life has been too easy?

Should I have spent more or less time drunk, passed out? Should I have never married that woman and stayed with her, had those children, sent them to those schools, settled in?

His songs are sweet, melodic. There's one with an image of a flower that lives only on this island and changes color at night from orange to white. A nice mystery, that one image. We can take it home with us when the ride is over. We can ponder what it means.

Later, at night, when I thought about how somewhere on the island the flower was changing colors, I heard the sound of trucks. There are trucks bringing in thousands of freshly laundered towels and trucks of mints and trucks of star fruit and kiwi and shrimp and bananas and trucks of steaks and bread and graham cracker crusts for pies and trucks of bacon and trucks of chlorine for the pools and trucks of rum and daiquiri mix and swizzle sticks and trucks of sunglasses and sweatshirts and trucks of ice cream and sand buckets and trucks of mangoes and salt and hair dye and trucks of gasoline for the trolleys and trucks of aloe vera in bubbling plastic. And while the trucks go on their secret way up and down the three-mile road, the flower changes color in the mangrove swamp, the swamp all chaotic tangled pulp, the color of squid, with roots hanging down from the branches and thorns sticking up from the ground like beds of nails. You can't veer off the road when you're driving these trucks, and the road is long and narrow. Paradise is fragile and surrounded on all sides by thorns.

It's paradise. Even the squall is beautiful. All the women have perfect golden hair, and the teenagers who ride the trolleys in the dark are gods and goddesses. Still, there's something not quite right about it. The golden hair, the yachts in the harbor glistening white like coffins, men drinking bourbon in their captain's chairs high up off the water. What is it?

This used to be a working plantation, the captain says. Eighty percent of the world's key limes were produced here. At night the trucks bring in hundreds of Jamaicans to put the towels on the racks of all the condominiums, to vacuum out the boats and serve mixed drinks at poolside. And you find yourself saying things the plantation owners might have said. I'm kind to them, they're happy here; look at how they're cared for, how they sing while they're working.

What is there to do at night? the teenagers ask the trolley driver. Not a thing, the driver says. Just go to bed and shut your eyes and sleep. When you open your eyes, the trucks will have brought you fresh-squeezed orange juice and coffee and the morning paper. Do you feel how quiet it is? Don't let it disturb you. Just let it come.

I wanted this section to be the color of those pastel paintings of children bending to pick up conch shells from the sands' edge, the mothers' dresses drawn in peach and aqua seafoam light. Today I saw those colors and grew oddly nostalgic for bronze and gray, for pumpkins and yellow and slate October Midwestern light that's a tincture of oak leaves, sycamore, silver maple.

Wednesday—
They're great jobs, my son says, taking the towels up and down the steps in paradise—better than working in some office in the Middle West sixty hours a week to save up enough money for one week you can't really afford on this island.

The men sit in the bubble at the top of their yachts all day long. The waiters go on and off the island. You think about race and class in ways you never have to think about them at home. A woman chips a shot out of a sand trap. A man rides a mower across the greens. The manatee blow bubbles in the olive-colored bay. Close your eyes and the world is the color of the Midwestern sky. Press your eyelids and it's the juice of blood oranges. The manatee swim, skin against skin, alongside their babies. The herons stalk their solitary prey.

Don't think I'm not grateful for this weather, the ocean, the hibiscus and blue sails, this rest from work. I'm aware that I've never done a thing to deserve it, that it could all be taken away from me, that there's a strain of something ugly running through every human system like a vein left inside a boiled shrimp. It's why we need to be forgiven.

Thursday—
Yesterday we saw a bird dive-bomb a cat that was threatening its nest. It was a ferocious bird, and all around old men were covering their gray heads and children were ducking. Today we saw three dolphins—a grandmother, mother, and calf swimming in the wake of a boat. And my daughter has fallen in love with babies. The paraphernalia: a baby's tennis shoe on a sea wall, a baby's citrus-colored floating tube, a baby's red sunglasses and white-brimmed hats and khaki shorts and skirted bathing suits— all human babies' things. But she also loves other babies: osprey babies and puppies and baby parrots sitting on rings in bird cages. She likes the human boy babies in baseball hats. They remind her of her brother, and she loves them.

This is the week all the Midwesterners go to the ocean. On television there are thousands of college kids singing karaoke.

I'd like to think about what it means to be a teenager on spring break, but I'm sunburned and windblown, and whatever brain I had has been baked out of me. I can't remember why I started this project or what it's for. I only know I've committed to continuing, like someone who's given up chocolate for Lent. But I have nothing I want to think about. I've been reading mysteries and taking afternoon naps.

My niece and nephew, twins, are spending the night with us to give my brother and his wife a break. Tomorrow's our last full day in paradise, where there's no reason at all to write.

Today we saw a rusted Toyota in the parking lot. Someone was gluing shells all over it with something that looked like peanut butter. I loved it, that someone would think of doing that and would stick to it, shell by shell. This resort is beautiful, but it's a completely invented tropical space like Disney World, the flowers and golf courses floating on imported soil. But the point is (and I'm tired) that I don't know how I ended up this week in this particular paradise. We'll be paying for it the rest of the year I've always loved the other paradise, the tacky Florida: the cars glued with shells, the colored spotlights on palm trees, the fake Polynesian gardens where you buy gods and glue in rhinestone eyes. I love the beach bars and the wax museums of famous criminals and motels outlined in purple neon and the plastic sippers you stick into an orange and the carved coconut heads and giant bags of citrus that you take home to the relatives in the trunk of your car. I love the first glimpse of the ocean after a twenty-hour drive, and all the people you recognize from home at the rest stops in Georgia. I love the hours of red dirt and the Stuckey's restaurants and the pecan orchards and the traffic around Atlanta and the brackish air and barbeque as you get near the Panhandle. The semi-rich shut down the pool at sunset and clap politely, and there are no steel bands or go-kart race tracks.

I started this meditation on the first day of Lent. I hope to keep going every day until Easter. Each day I go fishing in the water of this internal voice. This week the water's still, this angled pen a blue sail; the hook is lazy in the estuary, the water the color of lapis. So what if I don't catch a fish? I said that I would fish; that's all I promised. I bait the hook with each day's discipline. I have no guarantees that there is anything at all to catch in these particular waters, that something beneath the surface won't grab my pen and pull me under.

This is a privileged, protected bay. Out beyond these islands the sea gets rough. It takes stronger lines than I've brought with me, stronger lines than these.

Friday—

I've stood in a steel mill watching steel being rolled into hot aluminum, and the galvanized steel looks exactly like the strip of ocean through the two pine trees beyond my window—shimmery metallic liquid—the hot aluminum coats the palm fronds, the leaves of schefflera, the mirrored sunglasses of teenage boys.

Once I stayed at my aunt's house in the Keys, and at night the offshore boat lights would flicker and my uncle would flick the house lights on and off. They were bailbondsmen for drug traffickers. They wore buttery yellow, apricot, and aqua, ate saffron rice and stone crab.

I'm reading a crime novel about two women hit men, one of them a nihilist. We're all meat, the nihilist says, made out of chemicals, and at the end we go back to chemicals, so it doesn't matter what you do. She drills a hole in a victim's kneecap, and the screams are nothing to her, as meaningless and illusory as a single ocean wave; and I think this is Buddhism without the ethics—the non-violence, the focus on kindness and truth—the ethics are manmade, or at least that's how I've always understood it. I get the same cold feeling from it as from descriptions of the Greek afterlife. Why do you read books like this at the beach? Why are they always set here? It has to be something more than the fact that you have the time to read them.

I could see paradise as egalitarian—the metallic sun, the blue-green water, the blood red flowers and white sand, the Adir-ondack chairs and royal blue umbrellas, the babies in sundresses, and in the middle of it all, in the middle of metallic paradise, there's the criminal—yourself—whose soul is suddenly sucked away or has never been fully formed for this climate, and you're left glazed-eyed, cold, and utterly separate, paradise itself suddenly hard-edged, brittle, suffused with red, and you see people all around you but you can't speak with them.

— — —

In the gift shop I bought a copy of Anne Morrow Lindbergh's seashore book, that same solitary tone as *Walden*. Their solitude is at-one-with, atonement; the solitude I'm talking about here is something else entirely, and the fact that you can feel both of them, the metallic nihilism and the feeling of unity, means something, but the thing I'm sensing is that heaven and hell are less places than they are conditions of the soul. The nihilist in the crime novel I'm reading would say it's all chemicals and unimportant. I've believed that in my life but don't quite entirely believe it now.

I read some of Lindbergh's book on the beach, waiting for the sunset. The water was calm as glass, like a sci-fi landscape, and there were dolphins arcing a hundred feet offshore and beautiful children carrying pails of shells. A family with a daughter who looked like Audrey Hepburn and a grandfather wearing a sailor cap had set a tripod up on the beach. The father set the camera's timer and ran around behind them. He took picture after picture as the sun glowed red and yolk-like. A couple are getting married on the golf course; my brother and his wife are kind; my daughter is stunningly beautiful and innocent. Today we heard a chef play drums with a spatula and a knife against a grill while he sang and carved roast beef. We've talked to people from Croatia, from France, from Jamaica, from Korea, from Texas, from Michigan, from Wisconsin. A great blue heron dipped his feet in the pool while we swam. Some days the air feels like no temperature at all, like it's made for your body to walk through, your proper element. Love feels that way, feels just that easy. All day long a green parrot on the boat across the marina has been yelling "Edie! Edie!" We woke up this morning thinking it was a mother missing her child until we saw the green feathers swinging on a swing and heard "Edie Edie" in the same swinging rhythm.

Lindbergh's place was a beach cottage—no electricity, no one else around for three days while she wrote. The prose feels like clean sun and sand and has that saintly wholeness, that sense of journey and peace that you get in Thomas Merton and Thoreau, in May Sarton's journals and in Harlan Hubbard's *Shantyboat*. It makes my soul feel healthy to read it. It's earnest writing. Sincere.

There are demands on her time, so many of them from so many directions—children need things, and beyond that you are obsessively in love with them. I understand when she writes about multiplicity, about fragmented attention. I write a sentence in this journal and then talk to my daughter and then write another sentence. In almost every section there are gaps where life has entered into the spaces between thoughts. Sometimes the life takes me to the next thought, and sometimes it simply stops things. If I could have this notebook out in front of me all the time as I lived my life, I wouldn't have this odd need for secrecy. I'm not sure why I would write down everything I think and then feel somehow ashamed if someone in my immediate family were to pick it up and know what I was doing. Writing feels, in fact, like you've taken in another family member and haven't told them. I'm afraid sometimes that they'll feel as though I've abandoned them, or been lying all along. That the mother/wife daily me that they know so well is not the only me. That they'll think I've hidden something—and I have. This inner river is filled with "I," and the outer one is all functionality and "you." You're hungry/

sleepy/happy/sad; you need to brush your teeth, to eat; your hair looks beautiful like that.

It doesn't feel like that metallic separateness, though. There's a permeable membrane between the two selves. One wouldn't be possible without the other. The experience of love is grace.

All night long I dreamed, and I woke up from the dream knowing it was time to leave. The night sounded like rain. The boats were dumping bilge water into the harbor.

Saturday—
Breakfast with my daughter at the harbor, and we saw the last fins of the manatee, two cocker spaniels straining at their leashes at dockside, the almost invisible wires keeping the grackles off our food—eggs and toast and sweet strawberries.

Then a trip to the airport and a two-hour flight to go from the tropics to Indiana—where it's snowing and the sky is the color of diesel exhaust.

The manmade places here are abandoned warehouses and small industry and factory sludge, but the wild places we pass by in the car are beautiful—shadowed beech and oak. You can walk in the wildness here, and on Captiva the manmade places are by far more beautiful than the tangled swamps, (so you're tempted to think there that humans are far better artists than God, whereas here you know that human beings can make a mess of things and often do.)

— — —

My son is out with friends at the movies, and my daughter has been on the phone for hours. My husband and I went out to dinner, and it was, as always, the happiest I ever am—the way our own world closes in around us like a shell, and everything we think we say. It was this way from the first moment I saw him when I was eighteen and has never really gone away. It's so easy for us to be in this self-enclosed world, our children a part of it, this blessing. My childhood was difficult for me, and suddenly there at the end of it was this gift—hello! hello! The best thing I ever did, my grandmother said, was to marry him. And there are times I almost hate him, and times I resent the closed-in feeling, but more consistently there he is, the perfection rising up again over and over like an hour on a clock that you have faith will come around, if you're patient, again and again and again.

BOOK THREE: HOME

The Miracles of the Church seem to me to rest not so much upon faces or voices or healing power but upon our perception being made finer, so that coming suddenly near us from afar off, for a moment our eyes can see and our ears can hear what there is about us always.

—Willa Cather

Sunday

It's the Midwestern sky that's the problem. If you keep your gaze parallel to the ground, the landscape is lacy in the spring, as delicate as tatting, watercolor-like, a wash of green on the weeping willows, a wash of lavender and pink on the crab apple trees and redbuds, a wash of greeny white on the dogwood, marbled white bark on the sycamore. You can walk into the wild places and not be afraid the ground will give underneath your feet. The forest floor will hold you and the soft grass underneath the maple trees in the neighborhood.

But the sky! In the morning it was that milky opaque pale gray that I associate with Indiana skies all winter long, and in the afternoon, when the blue showed through, I realized that the gray was really a dirty white and the blue really a bluer shade of gray— always a bit hazy, a bit misted over, a little bit dirty, not ever really blue at all. Everything about it is subtle, including the odd attachment you have for it. A hazy love that you notice only in its absence. In another month the leaves will be budding, and that particular wash of green, so ocean-like, will color the air, particularly when the sky is white. White and gray are the background colors for an Indiana spring green. Blue might overpower it. You could almost believe in something. You could drown in its light.

Sunday night, the last waking hours before work and school begins again for all of us. This afternoon I saw Robby's mother out in the street, talking to a friend in a minivan. This is the end of spring break, and they would have spent it where? My guess is someplace along the Panhandle of Florida or Alabama. She's been at home for a week with all her other children. How can she let them out of her sight tomorrow?

My son spent the day at the computer. He got a new game in which he creates a virtual shadow self. Virtual Steve began with nothing, and by the afternoon he had an apartment with two televisions and one sink.

When virtual Steve went to the bathroom, which he did, he had to walk into the kitchen to wash his hands, and those extra steps almost made him late for his carpool. You need a sink in your kitchen, I told him, and he said he couldn't afford one and still have the two televisions, which he needed. In the afternoon he came downstairs to tell me he'd been promoted at work. It wasn't "he," it was "I." He said he could now afford the extra sink.

His real sister went in and watched her virtual brother go through his daily routine. She commented on his choice of clothes, the time of day he took a bath, the kind of car he drove.

At about four in the afternoon, my daughter came to tell me that the virtual Steve had met a girl, and he was scheduled to propose within the hour. I went upstairs to look.

She was a brunette. Where's she from? I asked. He said from Cleveland. He met her at work.

She seems like a nice girl, I said, and my daughter said she was.

When my son went to the bathroom later, he walked into the kitchen to wash his hands. We have two sinks! I said to him.

At night he came down from the computer, depressed. His virtual Steve was beginning to talk, he said. But I just burned down my house, he said. How, I asked. A fire, he said, from the new propane grill. Do you have insurance? I asked, and he said he hadn't bought enough.

I'm sorry, I said, and he said it was all right. He would just have to begin the game again tomorrow.

I thought I could smell a fire. So this is how it will be, I thought, for my grandchildren. Their virtual selves eternally impressed on silicone. You could transfer every act, every thought, at every point in your life somehow onto the computer. You could live forever, watching your television, burning your house down. Generations down the line could replay you over and over. Isn't that enough eternity for anyone? You couldn't be inside your skull and looking out, but still and all, there you'd be. And has anyone ever said that eternal life would involve sitting inside your skull and looking out? Knowing yourself as a separate I? The Sunday evening after a week's vacation in the South. Days of work spreading out in front of you. Your virtual self gets up and goes to the office. A part of you stays behind.

Years have gone by when I've lived like that, pushing my virtual self from here to there. The record I'm making of this Lent is in some ways a record separate from me as well—but in a richer way. And everything I see or hear makes not the virtual me but the one that witnesses feel more alive. I walk, I move from here to there more clearly at the center. Writing is all I want to do with my non-domestic life. Make up stories. Tell them. Begin again. Virtual beings springing out of the imagination as I've sprung out of some other imagination. Look. She washes her hands.

Grace

It's not just the weeping willows that have started to bud. That fragile green, the color of fresh snap peas, you can feel it on your teeth. It's that sweet.

The air is amazing. I walked out to the mailbox for the mail, and there was a neighborhood newsletter on bright pink paper. I read it as I walked back to the house, and when I looked up, I thought there was something wrong with my eyes. The air was absolutely the color of limes. The entire world was green underneath a sky the color of limestone.

When my friend Grace had her one and only mystical experience, this was the green she described. This experience of mine wasn't the least bit mystical—just a walk to the house from the mailbox, a color opposite the color wheel from the pink I was looking at, an Intro to Psychology experiment explainable by rods and cones within the eye, that's all. But still. How can you explain the mystery of the eye itself, of its reaction to color, its moist fragility working as it does in the midst of multiple universes composed of explosive fire and stone. The membrane of the eye. The fresh, mysterious green.

Two weeks away from Easter. I've written two hundred pages, and I still haven't told a soul about this. Because of my job, my friends and colleagues are mostly male, and this secret somehow allows me to hold them at an odd distance, though I feel closer to my husband in spite of, or because of, this other intimacy—and that may have to do with the content of this meditation more than anything, how I've grown to appreciate the equally fragile and lovely membrane of the home, its own wet cylinder, like a terrarium.

I take it back. I've told one person, my sister-in-law—because she revealed that she'd given up chocolate for Lent, and so I told her that I'd given up sloth. I've written every day, I told her, even in Captiva.

One night while we were there, my son fell asleep on the golf course putting green outside our window. He lay down on the green and looked up at the stars, so relaxed that he fell right into them. They were clear and hard as candy there, like the sky is supposed to look, and he was in awe of it. There's very seldom a night in a large Midwestern city when you can see anything in the sky beyond airplanes and satellites and radio towers.

My son is still bonded with the computer. I thought your house burned down, I say, and he says he was exaggerating. Just the porch burned down.

So, I say, are you married? And he says he was thriving in his professional life, not his personal one.

So she turned you down, I say, and he says his Sim isn't that good at relationships.

What does he do? I ask, and he says he's in internal affairs in the army. Soon he's going to be promoted to general.

Congratulations, I say, but what I'm thinking is why the army when you had all those other choices. The government lets you sign up for the army when you're only eighteen years old, and nothing your mother says can stop you.

The Sims are interesting for the usual ironic reasons. I get the easy rush of righteous indignation from the contrast between the live person at the computer screen and the simulated one, the connection between them, the way it makes you think about yourself as a Sim in both the material and spiritual sense.

But I think the real reason it interests me right now is because I'm writing this thing. Once it occurred to me that I would keep it up throughout Lent (and that's the oddest part of this, that it never really occurred to me that I wouldn't; that was never really an option), and once I saw that it was happening and that in parts of it I was shaping it like essays, and once I saw the way threads were appearing, and a structure, and I saw how I could manipulate those threads, could think of them like colors and be aware of the way I was knitting them together, and once it occurred to me that someone at some time might read it, then the hope I'd had at first—that there would be no disconnect between my authentic voice, that internal chattering, and the voice that comes out on the page, as though I were speaking only to myself or to God—became impossible. There is that sense in which nonfiction is less true than fiction. There are those things you don't talk about but that underlie everything you say. It's a simulated voice, a creation. You shape it. You hope it will take on some life and go, at times, where it wants to, so you can watch it. You hope it will take on a soul. At times you feel as though your own soul has escaped through some wormhole in time and wants to take up residence in the thing that you're creating. Like a planet you're escaping to on some rocket ship, some sci-fi thing, to escape a dying planet. You watch to see if the new planet has an atmosphere, if it has lakes and vegetation. You land your ship and open up the hatch and wait to see if you can breathe.

Wednesday Once Again

The vacation pictures are glossy with that wet membraney look, that feel I wanted the Captiva section to have, like that thin outline of blue you see sometimes around gray eyes. Though not a circle. I wanted it to be a vein or a slice, like turquoise in platinum, something like that. Like one of the sunset pictures in the middle of this gray-painted door on file cabinets that for twenty-five years I've called a desk.

I came home to a swamp. The front yard is a mud pit from the new sewer line, and the washing machine is backing up into the basement, and teenage boys and our dog are bringing huge hunks of dirt into the house.

It's everywhere. Our shoes are covered with it, and even when I get people to leave their shoes on the front porch, the dirt seems to cling to them and come inside anyway. The carpet on the stairs is nasty, and every inch of floor is covered with a fine layer of dusty silt no matter how much time we spend mopping. The plumber says it's the excavator's fault, and the excavator says it's the plumber's fault, and meanwhile mold is growing underneath the basement carpet, and yesterday when I cooked a roast the place smelled like a nursing home.

And this is all on top of the basic everyday squalor—my son dripping orange peels and cereal everyplace he walks, the laundry basket full of washed socks that we're too lazy to sort, and the everyday paper clutter.

There's chipping eye shadow dust in the children's bathroom—blue and gray with some kind of sparkly something that looks like it might not be good for any eye—and there's fish-food dust around my son's aquarium and plant dust underneath my husband's plants and dust all over the bookshelves when you remove a book, and there's a sticky film of dust on the kitchen cabinets and on the windows and the television screen, so that everything—the light from outside and from within computers and televisions—is filtered through a graying haze of dust. It's spring, and all of a sudden some environmental email list I'm on has kicked back to life, and I get daily ecstatic reports from people living on their mountains and their lakes and their Midwestern farms about what birds they've seen and what's budding and how quickly the snow is melting in Alaska and how beautiful the northern lights are, and everyone talks about The Creation! The Creation! And all I can think about is Decay!

And Lint! Whoever did laundry last emptied out the lint trap and left it in a ball on top of the washing machine, where it's mixed with spilled detergent and fabric softener into this sticky, disgusting goo.

So. It's Ash Wednesday all over again.

It's only supposed to happen once. I've been doing this for four weeks—two weeks to go until Easter—and I was supposed to grow, you know? Not walk around thinking that spring sucks because it's too damn muddy and my sewer isn't working right.

I would like to be all airy and optimistic and holy, but first let me get this out of my system. I feel, today, like blowing up my house and starting over again at the beginning.

Yesterday my entire family was in this mood. I blamed the squalor on my husband's plants and pets, and he blamed it on my old furniture, which he refused to glorify by the name "antiques." Ordinarily I would say *our* plants and pets and *our* furniture, but the lines are drawn.

Of course, we both know the main cause is that the front yard, including the driveway and sidewalk and our Japanese maple tree, has been attacked by a backhoe, but that knowledge doesn't really help when you feel powerless.

So, he said, looking around at the living room, what's all this chaos? Where did we get that chair? It was my grandmother's. And that one? My other grandmother's. And that table? My great-grandmother's. And that table over there? My great-aunt's. And that music cabinet? A great-great-grandfather. He brought it with him when he moved from Germany. And that dish? My great-grandmother painted it. And that picture? My great-uncle's mother was a missionary in China, and she bought it there. And that piano? You bought it for me when we were first married, I said, remember?

It's old! he said, and the bottom of the bench is falling out.

Get rid of it! he said. Get rid of it all. A giant garage sale, and then someone who can really paint will come in and paint the whole inside, and we'll have the floors refinished, and we'll get rid of the cheap curtains and strip off any remnant of wallpaper and have bare windows, and we'll sit in the middle of the white-washed rooms on the bare floors, and we'll watch that pile of mud in the front yard settle back down where it belongs.

Sounds good, I said. But can we just keep my great-grandmother's hand-painted plate with that note from my grandmother on the back of it and that chair that my great-grandfather signed and dated and that bed that your great-grandfather made?

OK, he said.

And how about the music cabinet? I can't stand to think of my great-great-grandfather bringing it all the way over the ocean, and then my grandmother filling it with her sheet music, and then me cavalierly selling it.

But you didn't even know him, my husband says, seeing where this is going and needing to get back to his original position. And by the time you get back into those great-greats, you've got so many different branches of families that didn't know each other and half the time didn't get along when they did, so how can you expect any of the furniture to match one whit? It looks like an old furniture store, he said. And just think how much dust these old finishes shed.

Just in this room alone, he said, you've got that ornate-looking Victorian thing over there, and you hate ornate, and four different-style lamps and four completely different-style chairs.

And I reminded him of the oak table I got from my grandmother and dearly loved that needed to be refinished because he'd put the guinea pig's cage on top of it, and the walnut table I got from my great-aunt that needed to be refinished because he'd put a leaking aquarium on it, and the antique rug that had a chewed place in it from when the dog was a puppy, and the plant stands that had made black places on the hardwood floor and that were now, even as we spoke, shedding dried leaves.

It's a draw, he said. It's a draw, I agreed, and we looked outside at the rain washing out the mud where the sidewalk used to be.

And so, it's another Ash Wednesday. I suppose I should be thinking again about my sins.

I've always been the one who gets the heirlooms. Our family has come down to just my brother and me, and right before someone goes, they seem to give me things, and in the giving it always feels like some attempt at immortality, some bit of love that went, misplaced or not, into the thing itself, a smear of soul. And so I have the Depression glasses, the amateur watercolors by friends of the family I didn't even know, and all the ill-assorted chairs, each the last one in a set, a line of chairs, the remaining DNA of that particular chair species.

Please understand. No one in my family has ever been anything more than middle-class. There's no family money handed down from one generation to the next—not a bit of it.

These pieces I'm referring to aren't particularly interesting designs; they weren't particularly important pieces in their time. They're the kinds of things that I could buy today at some thoroughly middle-class chain store. In fact, one of my grandmothers had particularly awful, gaudy taste. She collected cupids—damn fat little angels, my mother called them—and I've kept a particularly hideous one. It's her dining room furniture, in fact, that I've been oppressed by this past month, and she was the one who re-covered the pink and green chair in my living room, the one my husband was bothered by—as I can understand, believe me. I've got her thimble cabinet in our bedroom, and it's still filled with her thimbles, and now and then a thread will catch on my clothing as I walk by and it will unravel and spin like a button in a dryer.

So there are her dark mahogany things and my great-aunt's Victorian things and the simple maple pieces that belonged to my mother. Don't get me wrong; I've gotten rid of a lot of things. Last summer when my great-aunt died, I sat in her apartment with my father and stepmother, all of us throwing papers in trash bags, making piles for Goodwill to cart away. And when my mother died, I spent two weeks, every day from nine to five, going through each closet and each drawer. We had a yard sale. But still, I remember how proud my grandmother was of that silly chair, and on and on it goes like that until this house I'm living in is so filled with objects trailing memories and pieces of these other souls that I can't bear to part with them. Every time I look at that chair, I have this brief impression of my grandmother, and there are only a handful of us on this earth right now who remember her at all, only two of us who remember her with some certitude. If I can pass the chair with her note taped under the bottom to whichever one of my children becomes the archivist, then her memory will have lasted that much longer here, and after the hard and good work that was her life, she deserves that much.

Her name was Alma, which means "soul." One of the things I have from her house is an old white mug with ornate letters on the outside that read "Remember Me." How can I get rid of it, even though I have no idea who's being asked to remember whom? The pleader has been long forgotten. He or she should have painted his or her name on the bottom.

It's just the clash of all these departed souls that gets to me, the difficulty of holding them all together in my memory and making room for anything I've selected on my own. It's like creating a canon. Does this one go to make room for this one? Does Philip Larkin stay? Robert Lowell? Elizabeth Bishop? What happened to Longfellow? It's so difficult to live inside a time capsule. You have to keep expanding and expanding it to the edge of the universe to hold all these worthy souls.

Thank God the universe is expanding. It's just that I can't do the same with the walls of my house or whatever controls the memory in my brain cells. So what will I do? I have to pare things down. I have to keep a memory from everyone. I'll bring in some things of my own, though I have to say that my taste is, truly, as bad as my grandmother's. Somehow, though, I need to make room for both the present and the past.

Today we did some cleaning and some rearranging. You know, my husband says, I never noticed that the wheels on the bottom of that table look like shells. Unfortunately, I say, they do. I don't think it was intentional. And your ficus tree, I say, seems to be coming out of its winter funk. Still dropping leaves, he said. Well, yes, I said, there's that.

There will always be Ash Wednesdays. They seem to be as necessary to the soul as bread is to the body.

To the conservation email list: This afternoon, near the Monon Trail, I saw a mallard duck, that white line around his throat, his head a shining emerald satin.

Witness

God had to die, Nietzsche wrote, because Man cannot endure that such a witness should live.

What loneliness without the witness, even if it's only this quiet inner voice that echoes the witness of your own mother and father. Yes, you've done that well and no one else can see it, but I noticed it. I see you. Teenagers shut the doors to their rooms because of that uncomfortable feeling that their mothers can read their minds; that thing that was so comfortable as infants is suddenly impossible. Shut it out, that witnessing. Let me create my own world here, without your constant editing.

But I don't want to think about Nietzsche right now. I want to think about Pascal and the purpose of Ash Wednesdays scattered through our lives. "The Christian religion teaches men these two truths," he wrote, "that there is a god whom men can know and that there is a corruption in their nature which renders them unworthy of Him. . . . it is equally dangerous for man to know God without knowing his own wretchedness and to know his own wretchedness without knowing the Redeemer who can free him from it. . . . We can have an excellent knowledge of God without that of our own wretchedness and of our own wretchedness without that of God. But we cannot know Jesus Christ without knowing at the same time both God and our own wretchedness."

I don't know God. I don't know Jesus Christ. I mean that honestly. They're English words to me, containers, and what the words contain for me, what I've learned from culture, isn't anything I can believe in. What I want to understand is the mystery the words originally gestured toward as something living, something real. And then I need another word for it. Or I need the old words to be so rekindled with the mystery that I can use them without feeling as though I'm lying. "Lord I believe," Augustine wrote in the *Confessions*, "help Thou my unbelief." I would say I unbelieve, help now my belief.

I do, though, know my own wretchedness. I'm quite familiar with it. Wednesday after Wednesday I'm confronted with it. Maybe that's a start; maybe someday I'll know what the other part of the equation means.

I'm very aware of patterns as I'm writing this. I thought that I would cross the blue line in the center of the book and then move backward, touching again on the same subjects, like this: ABCDE—Captiva—EDCBA. Instead it seems Captiva was the scent of coffee beans in those parfait-shaped glasses they have at department store perfume counters, the ones you sniff between trying different fragrances.

If you've stuck with me this far, you can see where I'm headed. I'm still wearing the fragrance of Norway.

I have to say that I didn't choose the pattern. I have to say that I didn't even choose to notice it. That feels like a gift, like the pattern itself. (And yes, I did go to the mall last night to buy my daughter a belt she needed. It was the same mall where I went to get the socks the first Ash Wednesday.)

I didn't notice that pattern until right now, as I'm writing this. And I didn't choose to go there because I was conscious of a pattern. And I know the pattern can be explained psychologically, and I could perhaps despair at how little freedom I seem to have.

What I can choose to do, I hope, is to learn from it. So I'm not simply moving around in circles on one plane but lift myself up one step each time I go by a familiar landmark, so that I open the pattern up into an expanding spiral—a widening gyre, a Slinky toy, a spiral staircase—instead of digging a deeper and deeper path through repeated wear until I'm down so deep I can't see the sun.

My son's the only boy in the scrub orchestra, the one for students who never practice, the one where the conductor comes out and tunes the tone-deaf students' instruments.

My son plays the string bass, and when he wants to quit we remind him that this class is the A that averages his D in math and allows him to stay on the baseball team.

I listen to them tune up at the spring concert. The girls are seated on the stage in front of my son, their dresses a bright crimson satin, and behind them there's one of those optical-illusion backdrops that looks like a three-dimensional wall of light, a smoky lavender blue.

My son is wearing his father's suit and standing behind the girls and to the side.

When they dim the lights in the auditorium, his sheet music on the stand is a twilight-window-glass blue. It glows exactly like that, a twilight window, and behind him there's the sky. And all the red in the world is residing in those scarlet dresses. Crimson. They're ball gowns, and the girls look like a string of those red vinyl Christmas bells lit from inside by an incandescent bulb. My son stares at the rectangle of blue in front of him as he plays, as though the music really is transparent, as though he's looking through it to something I can't see.

Thresholds

Today's word is *liminality*. I've spent the morning and afternoon at work, listening to undergraduate papers on Yeats and Synge and C. S. Lewis and Anne Brontë, and at lunch there was a question and answer session with an Irish poet, Nuala Ní Dhomhnaill, and both Nuala and the students at one point or another said the word. *Liminality*.

It means threshold, but in the way in which it's been used today it has to do with luminous, with shimmering thresholds between worlds. Neither this world nor the next one, neither the past nor the present, on the threshold of something difficult to detect, but there.

The Irish poet talked about the reality of myths. "On the edge of my eye," she writes, "at imagination's quick, I sense the spots of a panther growing close."

I never think of the word *liminal*, but I think often of *lumen*—candle-lit. Last night when I watched the orchestra play, I wouldn't have thought of it that way. Underneath the light, the way the children burned with it, if it hadn't been, perhaps, for this threshold state I've been living in with this notebook and this pen, I know I wouldn't have, because when I sat down in the auditorium it was something I'd done so many times before, and I was thinking about what I'd get us all for dinner and how rushed I'd been to get there, and I was wondering whose shoes my son had borrowed, and I wasn't really looking at it or thinking about it as something I could write about. In fact, when there was a minute or two before the lights dimmed and I realized I could use that minute to get in my daily journal entry, my initial inner response was that there wasn't a thing in that auditorium to write about. It was the attention that the discipline of writing itself brings to the world around you that took me to the threshold, and I was so glad of it.

And I wouldn't have thought of it as a threshold, exactly, more like a privileged glimpse into a chapel, a domed room with colored glass windows lit from without by some source—either sun or stars or something else too bright to see, but outside of it, surrounding it and shining in—a shadowbox, glowing and mysterious, but not the least bit frightening.

There are no doors leading out of it, just the strong candy-colored windows and the one door into it—just one—where you can step in, look around, and be in awe of what you see. Those luminous beings with their flame-colored dresses and their fathers' suits, the lacquered bows and powdered strings, the instruments fiery gold, the harmony, the twilight window somehow all mythical and fragile, both transitory and eternal. And when the lights go up and the colors fade and you've seen the vision, you go to that one door, the one that let you in, and some quiet gatekeeper holds the door for you, easily letting you back out into the world again. As much as you might like to, you can't live there and still go home.

Now and then you get the sense that the people outside the chapel are flesh and blood, but once they step across that threshold they become part of the scenario itself—semi-transparent figures, opalescent glass, and they're for one moment stand-ins in some tableau. They let themselves be lit like that. Incandescence. Transfiguration. It's always there, but only when you look for it. Iconography. The correct words for "to paint" an icon are "to write."

And So

Tomorrow is the first day of Holy Week, and where am I? Instead of giving something up for Lent, I've added something, including pride in the fact that I've added it, unfortunately. But how do you separate the pride in, say, giving up chocolate and sticking to it for the entire season from the sacrifice? I suppose we're meant to fail at some level. It's built into human systems because they're human. There's always a hairline crack where evil enters in and breaks the system in two. A fault line.

Why? To keep things yeasty. The splitting of a cell. Why? Because something in the universe loves chaos and disorder. It has to be best to hold things together against the pressure on the fault line. Though sometimes I guess you have to just watch things fall apart. Otherwise you'd ignore the crack; you'd think you'd built something perfect when you hadn't.

Can you tell it's spring? This morning everyone in Indianapolis is out with a shovel digging in the dirt, bringing order to their gardens. Against the drift. Perhaps the chief end of man is to fight the battle against entropy.

Everything seems to participate, all living creatures. The birds picking up straw and mulch, the ants with their elaborate colonies.

But what I started to say is that in some ways this has felt like gluttony—a feast of chocolate, a feast of words. Not a sacrifice at all.

So I want to think about what I've sacrificed. Everything that takes up space in your life crowds out something else. So what's the something else?

Television, for one thing, that household god that turns the family into stone. Haven't watched it except while passing through a room. Though that hasn't been a sacrifice. Aimlessness, though that hasn't been a sacrifice.

What else? Gossip, idle complaining, downtime spent idly looking through catalogues, time spent listening to the radio, walking through malls. Still not sacrifices.

Some time with friends, lunch invitations. Time thinking about office politics, which is a strange and guilty pleasure. Because I spent time cleaning my office in January, I've been able to work more efficiently, so I've gotten things done that I need to. I've cut back on unhealthy and unproductive phone time, and at times I think that the purpose of this has been to create something so large and time-consuming in the center of my life that all my many sins have difficulty entering in.

I'm very tired, so I think I've sacrificed some resting time, and I know I've sacrificed exercise. I've substituted one discipline for another. Maybe sacrifice in human terms is another word for discipline. This feels like the discipline of meditation, a focusing. Sometimes prayer, sometimes confession, sometimes despair, sometimes praise. In some ways, though, I've sacrificed the comfort of lethargy. I feel some days as though I've run for miles.

All I'm doing finally is paying attention to the flow of words and recording them. It doesn't feel as though I'm creating these words, but rather that I'm writing them down and thinking about how to best display them. This blue glass here across from this blue plate, and here the lavender.

Why Lent? Why not Lent? All I know is that I couldn't keep this up much longer, not at this pace. Next Monday I go back to my old slothful ways. It remains to be seen whether this will have made a difference.

Frogs and Karaoke

Last night we went to an awards dinner at Butler and listened to a biologist give a lecture. It's always billed as a Last Lecture, a meditation on things that have been important to the speaker. This biologist has devoted his life to frogs because, he said, "I like them."

He brought a tape and played frog calls. Now and then he'd break in with an imitation, completely unselfconscious, to make sure that we'd heard some particular nuance. He wasn't interested in the sound because of what it meant; he was simply like a curator overwhelmed with the beauty and complexity of the objects in his museum. Tree frog. Salamander. Of course you've seen thousands of these, he said to us, if you live in Indiana, and all I could think was that I've never seen a frog or salamander in my entire adult life. So much for all this pride in my ability to pay attention. He showed us the difference in the pitch and how the female frogs were attracted to the lower-pitched sounds, the singers, and how other male frogs would attach themselves to the golden-throated ones to pick up cast-off females. The biologist taped the songs and experimented in the laboratory, and there were slides of sultry female frogs cuddling up next to Bose speakers.

After the lecture, we went to see Ken's secretary singing karaoke at the Eagles Club in Beech Grove. It was amazing karaoke, actually. Secretaries and construction workers and homemakers all getting up and singing like rock stars. Gorgeous voices and the high-fives and congratulations of all their friends. All week long you live for this singing.

Palm Sunday

There have been times, as I've been working on this, that I've felt that I was actually writing a book, that all these words were going to draw together into something. Even yesterday I felt somewhat buoyed up just by the process, by the day-to-dayness of it, and today it all crashed down around me and I realized that it was nothing. I'm talking to myself and looking in the mirror as I'm doing it.

This morning the twins next door were running up and down their driveway waving long strips of yellow paper, either practicing for or still under the spell of strips of green in church.

There are three televisions on in my house right now, the sound of buttons and zippers in the barrel of the dryer. Laura's in her Sunday evening funk over homework, and Steven's lost in an MTV dream.

I spent the afternoon cleaning out closets and the garage and sweeping dried leaves that had fallen to the floor from the ficus tree. Every time I turn around, another round has fallen. All I've done today is sweep. There are bags of old clothes and objects ready for the Goodwill truck tomorrow morning, and a pile of paint cans and old golf clubs and a set of broken crutches in the garage waiting for a hauler. I've sorted through books and linens. So many things I've given hours of my life to purchase, and nothing to show for it but dust.

Why palms? I don't get this story, really. Brush the threshold, sweep away the demons. Repeating the journey of the mother on the donkey. The children singing and their parents saying "Who is it?" I don't have a clue, I'd say to the twins if they asked me, but they won't. They'll never ask. They think they know exactly what they're doing. Their faces golden, and their hair, they run and leap and wave their paper fronds. There's something I can't even begin to see, tree branches brushing against the upstairs windows. I open them up to let in air.

Late in the afternoon on Palm Sunday, my daughter and I went to see the new Wal-Mart. I know. Pathetic of us, really. A strip of despairing blue-gray along the inside ceiling of this enormous building, what seems like miles of things you would never in a million years want to buy all arranged on shelves. You can't see outside, and the air has that depressing yellow-gray quality of the air right before a storm. The floors are concrete like the floors of an animal cage. We bought some shampoo because we needed some and we were there, but then we went right back outside. It was depressing, my daughter said, that ding ding ding sound and the voices telling you what's on sale and those signs up near the white pipes that cover the ceiling. Did you see those signs? she asked. Optics. Health and Beauty. Women. Men. There were signs on wires, and they were blowing from side to side as though they were reacting to some kind of weather. But it was all planned, my daughter said. There was a rhythm to it. They were like a shout. Optical! Optical! Everywhere there were money changers and plastic dolls.

The new Wal-Mart is right near our house. We had some kind of high hopes for it.

So much to do tomorrow. Long student papers to read, repairmen (still) to call, the children's homework to check, a car that needs a mirror replaced, phone calls and emails to return. Somewhere on my desk there's a contract that I've misplaced. It's tax day. Laura's got a report due on Guinea, and the entire family will get involved. There's baseball and softball. Who has time for Holy Week? I hear it's going to be raining for most of it.

These palms are messy. Sweep them up, please. Why are you

walking around with them? Monday's tomorrow, and we'll barely have time to breathe.

I take three trash bags out to the pile of things for the hauler. Once or twice a year we become so overwhelmed with stuff that we call him, and he comes here in a pickup truck with his mother. He has no teeth. Good Christian man, his ad says. For less than a hundred dollars, he takes our sins away.

— — —

My husband was in the garage arranging garden tools. He has faith that the mound of front-yard mud will become something. There are several boys, around nine or ten years old, playing basketball next door. One of them looks exactly like Robby, and we both notice it. It makes us sad this afternoon while we work. The grief lasted for about a week for us, the neighbors, and then it was buried and is resurrected now and then like this, glimpsing a boy with Robby's face setting a pick for his friend. It could be him, I say. It really could be. Some kind of visitation, though of course I don't really believe that. Though you hear of these things, I say, children coming back to give comfort to the ones they've left. But he should be down comforting his mother, my husband says. Maybe it's the neighborhood he's comforting, I say—the whole community, all of us who see him as he was, just walking out of two years ago right where he left off, in the middle of a game. It feels like that, my husband says, and something in you wants to run over and take the spirit boy, who will seem by that time like real flesh and blood, and you'll want to look him in the face. That bright, sweet, blue-eyed smile, and you want to say do you have any idea what's waiting for you if you continue on like this? It's Palm Sunday, six days before Good Friday, and he would say I know.

On Rivers and Cherries

All day long the light has been dimming; no blue in the landscape, no fire, until finally at five o'clock the day is heavy-lidded, reptilian. Everything is still. The canal isn't moving, and the surface is a deep green. The reflections of trees are so still they seem like a thick covering of moss or algae, like you could dip your hand in the water and it would come out coated with green shadows.

I come home and turn on all the lights. I light the gas fire to take out the chill. This morning I saw an old woman all bent like the handle of an umbrella walking to the Catholic church and eating soup out of a paper bowl. Thousands of fish that were killed in last summer's chemical spill in White River are apparently beginning to decompose. Their air sacs are rising to the surface of the river and floating like white balloons.

On Epiphany Sunday, whenever that is, I remember that you release balloons into the sky like carbonation, like the internal pressure of some true thing. But the light is dimming, and not a thing is released in me.

Though my house is, for the most part, in order.

This thing that's blown through me like the glass blower's breath as I've kept my appointment daily with this notebook is receding, I can feel it. Leaving what? A structure that once had some life inside of it. I can walk back through it when I wish, an old home, a discarded shell. The process has been, I think, a gift. I've wondered, at times, if I've gone crazy. I've gotten to the point where I don't care, really, and that in itself is a gift. This hasn't been driven particularly by energy but by discipline. I wanted to make one difficult promise in my life that I could keep even, and especially, when I didn't feel like it.

I'm going to try not to think of that. The pride starts to puff something up in me that bloats and rises like those air sacs on a poisoned river.

No, that's a little much, I'd say. I do have to say the process has given me a lot of joy. What has your writing given you? a student asked last week, and I said happiness. A gray, wet day, the dimming light. I sit here with a pen and notebook eating handfuls of sweet dried cherries. See what I mean? From poisonous rivers to cherries all because I've traveled through a paragraph.

And so I dive into the words and hold on to the conversation as though it might save me. From what? It's myself that I've always been afraid of.

Tuesday

Crab apple trees are in bloom. Passover begins tonight. Today is the closest I've come to breaking my vow. So busy all day long.

And besides, the crab apples chose today to blossom. Veils of white. I walked underneath them on my way to work, looked up, and thought of marriage. Or sex. Maybe just sex.

He's moved back home, the neighbor who fell in love and left his wife. His wife is beautiful and charming. It never had a thing to do with her.

It's just that you try to see the sky from underneath the flowering tree, the flesh and sinew of it, the wet bark and ooze, and the smell—it's enough to drive you mad.

This is the day when all you can see and all you want to see is the white trees, the ones that look like gauze and veils. It's that day. I'm sure you know it. There should be a name for it, like there should be a name for the day the leaves are at their peak in the fall or the day the green is first visible in the willows.

The flowering crab apple smell isn't sweet; it's patchouli and sandalwood and musk. The paper bark is scored and curled like tobacco leaves. The white is clean and stings the eyes, and the blossoms are cup-shaped, bell-like. At the tip of each branch the closed buds are pink as labia.

If you had been the one who married me, not her, you would have blossomed every day, he says; I know it. I'd sink down in the oceany blue of it, the deep red hue of it. Every day would be like this, not like my wife; nothing would ever stop me from this contemplation of the living, breathing God, which is what it feels like when he says, you wouldn't ever keep me from it, would you? You'd never refuse me?

And of course the other woman lies to him and says why no, if we lived together I would never, ever refuse you.

If religion is something more than empty ritual, if you want to feel that the universe has meaning, you have to take into consideration the intensity of this ecstasy, a circling around the thin lip of the petal, that edge like an ice skater's blade, the spring, and where else in the world can you feel it but on the petals' edge, once a year, today—this day—right before they fall to the ground and the leaves uncurl behind them.

Today I almost, almost broke my vow.

And what would it matter if I did? They're just words, vows are. I love you, I want to marry you. Say yes and yes and yes again until you're dripping with the scent of it.

I'm sorry. I was thinking about sex and then there were those trees. I didn't have much choice in this particular juxtaposition.

Midnight, Passover

Tonight I taught an evening class. The house is quiet as I'm writing this. Completely still. For a minute the voice in my head stopped. Like a clock stopped, and I just listened to the silence. It was like wine. Passover—I've never thought about it. But right now the house is so still it has that pre-holiday feel of the night before Christmas, like electrons have momentarily stopped their spinning and everything that breathes is holding its breath, like time stops and waits while something passes.

A hush. I didn't think of it but I felt it, feel it still. Every sound I make—the wineglass on the table, the brush of my sweater against the arm of the sofa, even the sound of the pen—breaks the stillness. Most of all the voice. Hush. Be still for one moment and know, etc.

Holiness. It has something to do with silence and with waiting. Listen. There it is. Do you hear it? Something's moving in the night.

At midnight I go upstairs to bed. The noise! The closet door, the lid of the vitamin bottle, the sound of clothes unzipping, of hose against my legs, of breathing, of light switches, of footsteps, of blankets. If you're locked in a soundproof room, the sound of your own breathing will drive you crazy.

I stand in my children's doorways and try to get the silence back. The soft sounds in there are comforting. I understand why the children rid the house of leavening the night before Passover. Anything that rises high enough might call too much attention to itself. Tonight's the night you don't want to be the first in anything. Midnight's past, and it's passed us by again. You're unbelievably grateful for the blessing.

Wednesday

I spent today typing up other days. Does that count as writing? Probably not. Three sentences now today, the ones you've just read, and now this one. Does this count? Technically, I suppose. The letter of the self-imposed law, but not the spirit.

In order to keep a discipline, sometimes you have to find the tiniest hole in the day when the lens has squeezed itself almost shut—the iris diaphragm constricting, blocking out the light. You have to thrust forceps inside the space and pry it open in order for anything at all to be born through that tiny aperture.

Which makes me think about Schrödinger's cat, which has something to do with a space as small as the tiny space through which I have to project a world, a pinhole in this day, to write.

How many books have I read about quantum physics, and why do I still not understand it?

Besides the fact that I'm so bad at math, of course.

It has something to do with the fact that at some subatomic level an electron has a fifty percent chance of being either a particle or a wave, so that nothing is at some level really anything you could hang your hat on. And there's all this empty space between electrons like the space between the stars. Do I have this vision of the universe correct? Is this the proper backdrop for my one and only life? Do I have it right? Probably not, but I'll keep going here because it's what we all believe.

And so. Once this thing has been observed as either a particle or a wave, it's fixed and is what it is forever and ever. And so we love to think that human life is essential in the universe because we observe things, and in so observing we say what these things are. Lights! Camera! Action! At every moment we create what is.

Though there's the other theory where those electrons prior to being observed haven't declared themselves, and the ones we can observe are the ones that have declared themselves, have made a commitment, a leap of faith, are walking down the aisle toward marriage, graduation. I am a particle, and what we're observing is its history. We're history writers rather than reality creators.

It's important that we get this right. Everything seems so old and predictable, and then there's a whole new paradigm and life seems interesting again.

"The more dangerous a subject," the physicist Andre Linde said, "the more interesting it is." He sees our universe as a giant inflationary bubble with other bubbles rising up alongside and out of it, blowing up like pink bubblegum, the whole thing like the bubble rising and popping from a bubble pipe. Each bubble owes its birth to another and to another, and "the history of the cosmos," Timothy Ferris writes, "is darker than the depths of the sea and its myriad futures richer and less predictable than all the unpainted paintings and uncomposed songs yet to emerge from the minds of all the humans to be born from now till the sun goes red and dies."

Quantum experiments involve shooting photons through an aperture and bouncing them off of mirrors, and the strange vision of the universe that results—the observer changing the observations or creating parallel universes where all potential states are true simultaneously, or a glimpse of the universe as one interwoven thing where all potentialities connect and there are no deep, mysterious spaces of emptiness and dark matter between the stars or between the parts of an atom. All that empty space is something filled with what is and was and could be, and the distance between this place and time and God is not an empty distance.

"But the universe was not always big and classical," Ferris writes. "Once it was small and quantum and possibly it has not lost the memory of those times. . . ."

I love the theory that God made this universe as a creative one, that He wanted to create surprises for Himself, that it's a universe impossible to predict, and that we ourselves are unpredictable and creative, making universes with the imagination.

We like to think that what we do has some eternal meaning. Scientists think their observations help create reality, and writers like to think that image- and world-making is God's primary talent, that God is a particularly amazing novelist.

Thursday

Some days I feel so limited by these five senses, by my position in time and space, by my particular size.

It's Maundy Thursday afternoon, four o'clock and dark as twilight. The windows in my house are a deep sea green. It's the first spring storm. The streets are flooded, and Tuesday's white flowers are falling all at once in the strong wind, blowing horizontal to the ground like winter sleet.

I've turned the lights on inside the house. There's a stream of rising bubbles in an aquarium that's lit by a nearby desk lamp, and the stream of bubbles looks, I swear it, like a candle flame. I catch a glimpse of it out of the corner of my eye and look again, each time to make sure the water's not on fire, like the Holy Spirit, whatever that is, is blazing up from some goldfish in the middle of this landlocked city that's turned, suddenly, as thunderous as the ocean.

All the electrical wires outside the house have turned silver with rainwater. Inside the house it's warm and tight, and the lamps turn you inward.

Tonight I'll cook, and we'll eat in the kitchen by candlelight. I'm sitting here reading science, still.

I've been thinking about photons split in two and communicating over vast distances, about all that quantum weirdness, and wondering if there is much difference finally between human beings and things as small as that, whether there's consciousness in all things, a connection between all things, if that metaphor of a wasteland between cells, between parts of atoms, between heavenly bodies and human beings, has in fact been the wrong metaphor and makes us see ourselves as extraordinarily isolated when in fact we're not.

My daughter has a new green Easter dress, a polished cotton, like chintz, and she came down in the living room to turn around for me while I was reading, like a whirling globe.

I feel, she said, like a girl in one of those old movies who stands up on a chair and turns while her mommy sits on the floor with pins in her mouth to fix the hem, and there are children all around her and the daddy's at the table with the checkbook. I feel just like that girl, she said.

Today her science teacher spilled a glass of grasshoppers on her lap, and the smell of formaldehyde almost made her gag. She didn't mind cutting into one later, fixing it to a board with pins, she said, and peering down inside, the subatomic light striking her eye, deciding in that moment whether to behave as a point or a line, to wear this dress or that one, to have the hem at this or that length, to wear the green or red, and in that moment eternally to wear that dress in every Easter photo from this particular time and place and never ever any other. And if it can't decide, it never is anything but what it could have been—a girl locked in her bedroom, trying to choose.

Good Friday

So I began this meditation reading Augustine, and I seem to be ending it reading science and realizing that in all of this I'm looking for those moments when the world stops. Or rather, not the world, but my own furious spinning in the world becomes so harmonized with the music outside of it that it feels like singing. But not singing, the part of music that lies between the notes, the silences that give each piece time to resonate and fade. Those holy moments when all you feel is awe. The silence of Passover, of Christmas Eve, of the moment before the orchestra begins playing, of my neighbor looking out her living room window, of my daughter in her new green dress, of candles lit in memory of a boy's death in a chapel filled with history.

This house on Good Friday morning. Liminality. Lumina. Moments of grace when everything surrounding them is preparation.

Light.

When a photon drops down one shell in its rotation, and then another, it's out of weariness. But in that weariness a spark of light blazes. In our own weariness, perhaps we do the same.

What's the difference between the holy silence of the night before a holiday and the eerie silence of an empty, unlocked house at night? I suppose it's faith. In the benevolence of things that you can't see or even begin to understand.

Saturday

It rained all day Good Friday, and today the sky is, again, a lacquered blue. I see a boy and girl on the shoulder of the highway, kissing. They're dressed in black, their hair dyed raven feathers with burgundy stripes. So hip and cynical, and still, on an early spring day, they're fused together like butterflies or any other winged insects over a heated summer pond. All through Broad Ripple, along the trail, there are humans glued together like this, transparent as leaf-green wings, colliding in midair.

So what have I learned from this meditation? Something about how rich the world is. During Holy Week in particular, I've for some reason been more aware of the flame of the soul in every face I see, how rich the fire, the blazing faces. This party, this family, this community of faces. A sense of oddly candled eggs, that jeweled Easter diorama sense that there are lenses everywhere that you can look through into that home, this soul, that cell, or this expanse of sky. And that everywhere you look, in any direction, there would be equal riches. The universe is constant in that way. The sense of holiness is a real sense, and religions and places have found a way to make that feeling visible when you can't call it up readily, like a sheet thrown over a ghost, a spirit. You find the rituals and architectures that make that holiness most evident to you. The best stories are filled with windows into the real.

— — —

The cups are ivory with a rim of silvery blue where your lips would touch them. The blue rings float above the kitchen counter—six rings—and there are beads of white light floating on the rings like stars. They orbit the cups, these stars, on their blue rings around six pools of color.

I'm dyeing eggs. From where I sit across the kitchen table

writing, I can't see the tinted water, just the white cups' rims, but I know the water's there. I know that each cup holds an egg. In a minute or two I'll dip a spoon inside each disc of color, and the egg will rise out coated with the jeweled tints of Easter.

The egg goes in the water pale as bone and rises through the galaxies coated with fiery metallic reds and blues and yellows, the color of stones and stars and bicycles and popcorn bowls and fish and sun and light. Rose quartz, emerald, topaz, sapphire, ruby, garnet, diamond.

Why am I dyeing eggs? My children are teenagers, out with their friends tonight. I suppose I'm doing this because I want them to wake up in the morning and remember that they're children. I want them to rise up from their beds like they're swimming up through crystal blue-green water, breaking through the disk of night, their bodies streaming colors until they're coated with them. I want them to have this day, brief glimpses of holiness and mystery, so they can look for other days like it in other places and know something about love. This world could have been designed without love, but it wasn't.

I focus on the discs of colored water and then the rims of the six white cups, and suddenly all I see are the floating circles. The rest of the cup fades, and then the discs, until it's only the rings, once again, that spin above the counter. One slight shift on my part, one choice, one conscious focus of my eye, and there they are again, the white cups on the counter filled with water and dye and the sharp tang of vinegar.

Another conscious choice and the luminous rings are the only things I see. Every year of my life, as I colored eggs, they were there in front of me, silver and eternal, waiting to be seen.

What do I know at the end of these forty days? That vision is a gift of discipline.

Sunday

Why is Easter so late this year, two weeks after the school holidays, in fact, long beyond the daffodils and tulips? Is it just arbitrary?

I have no idea, so I look it up.

Easter occurs on the day of the first full moon after the vernal equinox, the day the sun crosses the equator, dividing the days into equal parts darkness and light. From this point on, in the northern hemisphere, the days will get longer.

In our calendar Easter is tied quite clearly to the seasons. We have a lunar calendar, and leap year, which happened this February, was begun to keep the Christian holidays fixed within the seasons where they belong, which is to say within the correctly resonant ones.

The Islamic calendar is solar, and Ramadan rotates through the year. But Christian holidays have that pagan edge, that connection to the seasons, the winter locking-up and springtime ooze. In church they gave the children bulbs to plant on Easter morning.

But it's stranger than this, in fact, and far more complicated. I dive down into the dictionary and discover things I didn't know, words like *golden number* and *paschal moon* and *epact*. It's all part of the Metonic cycle, a period of nineteen years after the lapse of which (according to the dictionary) the phases of the moon return to a particular date in the calendar year. They started this calendar on June 24, 432 B.C., and it was named after a fifth-century Greek astronomer named Meton. Easter is the first Sunday after the paschal full moon, which may be quite different from the actual full moon.

And what's the paschal moon? It's the lunar month whose two

hundred and fourteenth day falls on or next to March 21, which is a rule that follows the golden number, which is the number of a particular year, a numbering that started in 432 B.C. and goes up to nineteen and then rotates through again. So the year 2000's golden number is six, and the year 2001 is seven, and the year 2002 is eight, and the year 2003 is nine, and so on up to nineteen, when it begins again with one.

This amazes me. Just think of it. In 432 B.C. someone started counting at one, and the counting hasn't ended, one year leading to the next, all of them connected together almost arbitrarily, by the passing on of a story. The golden number of 2000 is six, and its dominical letter is BA, which has to do with a lettering of months that goes back eons of human time as well. The epact number is twenty-four, which is the number of days' difference between the lunar and the solar year or the age of the ripe moon at the beginning of the calendar year, which is also called the menstrual age.

It's all both arbitrary and careful, both scientific and superstitious. Whatever it is, it shows how much human beings have believed that there is some order to the universe, that it can be apprehended and understood, and how much we've lived our lives accordingly. And how odd that in this, the first year of another century, in a provincial city in the American Middle West, we should wake up one morning and, looking at the calendar, know that it's time to put on our Easter clothes. We knew nothing about the paschal moon, and still my daughter spins in her new dress in the living room.

Of course I feel there should be some further revelation here. But the house is quiet. The children are still asleep; my husband is playing golf on the computer. A cardinal sings by the bird feeder. I head toward some insight, and then the dog barks at a passing dog, the dryer signals that it's done drying, and all I feel is annoyance.

This week I've been reading science, I've gone back to Augustine, I've been reading a theologian on the death of God, I've looked up the Easter calendar. I'm nearing the end of this meditation and want to learn as much as I can. Last night while I was waiting up for my children, I skimmed through a book of sacred writing, thinking here, it may be here. I'll find the answer here. I read Paul's letters to the Corinthians, and so much of it seemed like background noise to me—politics, the barking dog—and then something would open out into something deep and true—if I have not love, I am but a . . .—and then it would turn to noise again. A radio station that was so far away it was nothing but static and now and then an intelligible sentence, a place where the words became a clear window into something beyond them, which is of course what, at their best, you want the words to do. Not to point, but instead to magnify, to see down into or above, to serve as another sense beyond these limited ones.

— — —

The hummingbirds come back this week, my mother-in-law said. They always come back on Gladys's birthday. She told me that one year, and sure enough, every year they're hovering around the feeder in time for Gladys's cake. No golden numbers, no special calendars; they just return on the 28th.

The air smells like cake today, my son says, and he means it.

We went to my brother's church for Easter. On Easter Sunday I don't have to make any decisions. This is simply what we do.

My sister-in-law wore red; my stepmother wore coral. My daughter and father wore sunflower yellow, and my son and husband and niece and nephew wore bright blue. I was going to wear my normal black, but my family was horrified, so I dressed in beige. I'm not a flamboyant person.

The sky wore its accustomed gray. The church was dim, like you were looking at the place through smoke, and it was filled with old people. My daughter and I were depressed by it. It's all about death, she whispered to me. I felt it pull me down.

This church was designed to rely on natural light, and the day was dark; it was a Methodist service filled with plain speech. No interesting rhetoric, no interesting music, a children's choir so small they recruited an adult soprano so that you could hear them at all.

The minister gave his sermon with his Mississippi voice, all awkward narrative.

' As it turns out, it was his last Easter sermon. He's retiring, and his voice caught as he talked. I've never told this story, he said, and for the first time in his life, he said he wasn't allowing the church to make a tape or write the sermon down. It was more moving than usual, I thought, because he was so passionate and heartfelt, because he was conscious of this as his last formal words. It seemed to be his natural voice.

On the way to Columbus later, my son said the sermon was interesting. I'm a philosophical guy, he said.

It's all about how he was going to die, my daughter said, and it was boring.

He's not dying, my son said. He's retiring. You didn't listen. And anyway, it was metaphorical.

Early in his career, the minister had gone on a silent retreat where they used images to meditate upon. For thirty days he didn't talk. By the last night he hadn't felt anything, he said, and so he went into the chapel and told himself he would stay up the entire night until something happened.

He meditated on the cross, then felt a blinding terror. And he tells the story well, step by step, as he decides to fight the terror and at its worst point gets up onto the cross with Christ. At that point he finds himself in the tomb, where the two of them laugh and joke like kids at summer camp, and the terror is gone; and when he feels ready, the two of them walk outside into the sun.

It's the Easter story, and of course I think sensory deprivation and hallucination, though I'm moved by his telling of it and by the strength of his belief, and by, in particular, the courage he felt he had to muster to tell it, and by his face earlier in the hour when he baptized an infant, his last baptism.

It's Easter, near the end of this meditation, and I want a turn here toward the light. Maybe you can sense that I'm feeling the need to do that. But the day was dark and raining, we all had the beginning of some flu, we ate too much that afternoon, and all the songs on the radio as we drove to Columbus erased any lingering sweet innocence.

Oh, I could turn if I tried to. And I'll still try to. Like this: The green was a curtain. Our family was together, and my husband mowed his parents' grass for them, and the smell was sweet. My children were kind to their grandparents, and my son told his grandmother the minister's story. There was peace in this family and in this part of the world on this particular Sunday after the paschal moon, and all of it was good. And we spent the afternoon watching basketball and eating coconut pie in the warm interior of the house in the middle of the country with people we loved, and every Easter Sunday from now until I die will be layered with the memory of this particular one, no matter what happens in the intervening years.

In the morning we had passed the Strickland house. They were getting in their car for church, the remaining son and daughter in their Easter clothes. They will never be through with their grieving. Every Lent, it will return with equal force to them.

This day feels like a pause, a rest in the middle of sorrow. My husband's father is the sweetest man who ever lived. He showed us before we left how his feet have swollen. Congestive heart failure. He's in his eighties. My children love him with every fiber of their being. I want to believe that that love will continue. I want to believe that love itself is a window into eternity.

In less than a week the hummingbirds will return to the backyard feeders. The sugared water will glow red in the afternoon light. This particular day is done now, layered into time.

THE JOY OF ALL WHO SORROW

Therefore, paint on wood and present for contemplation Him who desired to become visible.

—St. John of Damascus, "On the Divine Images" (1239)

1

Summer, 2002.

I still have months and months to go before my Mary is redeemed. This time I'm in the advanced class, with those who have left and returned and those who have made this a part of their lives. Marussa is in the class, working on her second icon. This time the Archangel Michael with his difficult gold-leaf hair. The meeting with her teacher went well.

I get ready to paint a line. Really look before you begin, Mother Catherine says. She points to the robe I'm about to paint. She has me look at the prototype and also at her sleeve. See how the shadow of a fold of cloth runs down one side and then hooks like an umbrella around a line of lighter cloth? Look at this. See how there are umbrella handles running up and down my arm? The process of learning to paint involves learning to see double. The process of learning to write, Flannery O'Connor said, is the same. It's all in learning how to see.

Mother Catherine and I talk about writing and painting. I used to think these iconographic images were simply poorly drawn, I say, grotesque and odd—cartoons.

The human faces you think are real, Mother Catherine says, are sometimes nothing more than the projection of a social self onto a screen. We're fond of living in illusion. To see the real, you sometimes have to enter this strange shadowless place of hard lines, of vermilions and blood reds and ochres.

Sometimes, I say, as I've gone through this past three years, I've looked at people when they didn't know I was looking at them. You have to catch the face when they don't know they're being watched. And I've seen them everywhere, I tell Mother Catherine, these mysterious icon eyes peering through the eyehole of the human face.

And oddly, as I begin to paint my icon, I begin to see other faces in Mary's face. Sometimes I see my great-aunt, sometimes my mother, and sometimes Robby. And others who have died: My husband's uncle Wayne Dale Neville. My son's friend Susan. My good friend Dale. And my good friend Jackie. All these eyes looking out through the icon eyes as I begin again to paint.

2

I have to practice my strokes on a sheet of paper. It's always brighter, Mother Catherine says, at the end of the stroke. Chromium oxide green and ochre. *Salvation is precisely salvation from shame.* I make mistakes. Cadmium orange. *Sinners are not mistakes. This is what the demons want us to believe. Sinners are feverish children, who in their delirium often project onto God the rejection that they have received from others.* Chromium oxide green and ochre. Cadmium orange. Burnt sienna.

3

Yours was the green class, Mother Catherine says.

Because I stopped and started and stopped again, and because I had six weeks' worth of highlights to layer on Mary's face before I could get to the end—the crimson line around the gold leaf halo, the white lines around the crimson line, the Greek lettering and the stars on Mary's robe—I've moved away in time from the green class, the color of Ordinary Time.

It was, in fact, she said, a difficult green. It had a tendency to mar the board. It was difficult to keep it even.

It was a beautiful spring leaf green, and I'd wanted it too, but ochre, Mother Catherine said, is more reliable, and since I'm the last one in the class to finish, and by my finishing I will have helped create a class where everyone saw this project through, I go with ochre.

Though when you puddle ochre, Mother Catherine says, just be aware that it tends to want to run ahead too quickly.

Each color has its temperament, she says, like a breed of dog.

— — —

I paint the background, then work for a week practicing my Greek lettering before I touch the board again. *Mother of God,* I paint in crimson in some language I can't begin to read.

I paint the edge of the board with iron oxide. Two, three coats. Across the room there are three African women working on Ethiopian icons, and Mother Catherine offers her instructions in their language. She moves around the room, from the group of three to the two women who are working on icons for an Episcopal church, to Len, who sits in front of a desk covered with four boards and the mess of white gesso, to Marussa with St. Michael, to James, age eighty-nine, who's working on an icon of John the Baptist, and back to me. Mother Catherine! Mother Catherine! we call. We're all like children. Did I do this right?

It feels odd to me to be painting over the red slashes from when the freshly gessoed board was blessed. They're still there, Mother Catherine says, underneath. They always will be.

When the slashes were first made, I thought they were the color of blood, but the iron oxide red is the true color—deeper, unoxidized blood, despite its name, the kind you see in the tubes at the doctor's office.

You're on the home stretch, she says; you're almost done.

4

It's Mother Catherine's birthday, and we're having a party. It's my job to bring the fruit.

I purchase a bouquet of daisies made from pineapple and cantaloupe, tulips made from strawberries stuffed with marshmallows. I feel good being able to bring this gift. I feel like one of the Magi.

Around noon on Saturday I show up at the door to the monastery and ring the bell. No one answers. I go around to the side door and then around back, through the alley, through the rusted gate, through the vegetable garden, onto the screened-in porch with the torn screens. I try that door, the one closest to the kitchen. No one answers.

I sit for about an hour on the front porch, holding my strange basket of flowers. I don't mind waiting. A man walks up carrying an icon wrapped in felt. I've never seen him before. He sits down beside me for a while. No class? he asks. It turns out he's missed about a year of classes but is ready to work again. He shows me his icon. It's Christ. Achingly beautiful. I'd be afraid to attempt that, I say. He says it's his sixth or seventh icon, that he met Mother Catherine when she was working an anti-slavery booth at Black Expo. I notice for the first time that the icons are not any particular race, that you can see yellow in the face, and red and shades of brown and white around the eyes.

After a while he decides to leave, says he'll be back the next Saturday. He's waited this long to return; he can wait another week or two or three. He hadn't known about the party. I'm sure that I've got the time wrong, I say, and I'm content to wait a while longer.

I wait another half-hour or so and then put the fruit flowers in the car and walk around the corner toward the Joy of All Who Sorrow.

I ask in the bookstore if anyone has seen Mother Catherine, and the bookstore manager says no, but that I might check in the church itself. Maybe the party is in there. And for the first time I go inside.

The church is filled with the smell of incense. A young couple stand up near the altar, talking with a priest. The woman is dressed in homemade clothes, a kerchief on her head. The man is wearing a white shirt. I feel as though I've walked into an icon, the odd mixture of gloom and light, the earthy colors. The three of them stand surrounded by paintings of the saints, the stations of the cross, by embroidered curtains and cloth, reds and browns like the inside of a womb, a cave. The three people standing there, the young couple and the priest, feel like one of the paintings made flesh. When they turn to look at me, I can see it, as I've learned to see it, in their eyes. The social masks are gone, and there are the icon eyes again. Something has happened. I don't belong there. I walk back to my car and to my silly-looking stalks of fruit, and drive on home.

Later that day I opened my email and found a message from one of my classmates. The party had been rescheduled. There had been a death in the parish, a baby girl. The couple I had seen were the mother and father. They'd lost their first child. The priest was comforting them. The rest of the community was in the common room, waiting to join them in their suffering.

— — —

This is the first time we've had a party in this house, Mother Catherine said, as she looked at the group of us seated around the table. Bev and Gale brought vegetarian Chinese in boxes, Len brought brownies, Claire brought ice cream made from rice, and Marussa brought an altar cloth she'd embroidered as well as three homemade pies. Mother Marcaria was there, and it turned out that her birthday had been the week before. So now we were celebrating two birthdays, and it felt warm and festive around the table.

There were others at the table that I didn't know that well by name. Ellen? Josh? John? Margaret? Joann? James wasn't there, the one who was working on John the Baptist. He'd fallen ill and would die within a month, though at the time we didn't know that.

I'd ordered a second bouquet of fruit, and it sat in the center of the table, attracting fruit flies. Late August, and that's what fruit tends to do.

Marussa had called her mother earlier in the week. At that point she was planning to bring only two pies. This threw her mother into a fury of Orthodox mothering. Marussa started getting calls from her brothers. Two pies! the mother was saying to everyone who would listen. Two pies! Were there two doves released from the ark? Are there two members of the Holy Family? Are there not three in the Trinity? No one brings two pies to a monastery, and so Marussa had made a third one, some kind of amazing walnut-crusted thing.

She entertained us with her Orthodox mother stories. There are elaborate instructions for washing the altar cloth. The wash water has to be saved, because by being touched, the cloth has been made holy. The cloth touches the water, the water touches the earth, the earth touches the tree, the tree is made into a table, which is as ugly as my grandmother's but which is made beautiful by the group of people sitting around it and which is, I realize now, the thing my grandmother's table was missing. My grandmother, my mother and my brother and my father and all the cousins and aunts and uncles and friends and spouses and neighbors and colleagues and their children, growing older and away, away, the thing that I've been grieving, these celebrations stopping time, celebrating in the face of sorrow.

5

And so. On the day in October, three years later, the very day that the race cars run and the movie stars descend on our city, I sit in the basement of the monastery, paint still peeling from the outside walls, the ancient appliances with their fraying cords in place, the jars of hardened egg and lost brushes buried under sketches and books, and I hold a cup of warm oil over the completed face of my Virgin Mary.

This is the part I love the best, Mother Catherine says, and I say it's the part I've been dreading. While Mother Catherine prays, I hold my breath and close my eyes and pour.

I remember every story about icons disappearing under the oil, about beginning over. I couldn't do it, I think. Three more years. It's impossible. I couldn't do it.

When I'm done pouring, I look down at the icon on the table.

The first miracle to be attributed to this icon. Despite my lack of faith, the colors held. The second miracle? It was the way the face really appeared to emanate light now, in the same way that the pattern of wood is clarified by the rubbing in of oil.

For three hours I wait for the oil to dry, then rub in more, lightly, until I cover once again every portion of her face, until the shadows become real shadows to me and the bonnet a real bonnet, and the light, which I know realistically is due to craft, to mixtures of lighter colors and to certain brush strokes and to a tilting of the board, that light becomes real light, something mysterious and true.

When I leave the monastery that afternoon, I leave my Virgin Mary glistening under a purple light. Underneath a light, like a newborn baby in a crib. During the week, Mother Catherine will go in periodically to check on her, to add oil if she seems to dry unevenly. My Mary will remain there until she's ready to emerge into the harsher light of day.

— — —

On a Sunday, two weeks later, I head to the Joy of All Who Sorrow. Walking back into the holy gloom, running a little late, I realize right away that I've done something terribly wrong. My icon lies up on a table waiting to be blessed, and I don't belong here. I have no idea what I'm supposed to do.

I have no head-covering. I-I-I. Couldn't I for one second have let go of the fact that my presence here was important because it was my icon waiting to be blessed and thought about the fact that this church was Orthodox?

I stand at the doorway, late, remembering back to the days before Vatican II when I would go with a friend to a Catholic church and there would be handkerchiefs or scarves on a table by the door.

I look around for something to put over my hair, and there's nothing. I don't know whether I should leave or stay.

A woman in a blue denim skirt comes up to welcome me. She has a beautiful smile. I point to my head, and she removes her scarf. I'll go hatless too, she says, it's all right. It doesn't matter. Really. Come in, she says. Sit down.

And so I do.

Running late, moving from the bright October daylight to the medieval gloom, sitting down next to the smiling woman with no head-covering, I wasn't prepared for my reaction, and it took me by surprise. Everything was so extraordinarily beautiful, including the woman's kindness, that I started to cry.

But it was more than simply the act of kindness; it was something about the ritual, which contained a motion that stretched back through time, like a golden-hued intricate machine, a Victorian toy. I can't explain it. It was a time capsule, all movement, and I only know that I'd never seen anything like it, the way these beautiful children, miniature adults, circled with their parents and their grandparents so sweetly from icon to icon, the deep bows of veneration, the prayers and candles, the theater of it all— the way the curtains closed on the bread and wine when they were just that, bread and wine, and the chanting of the priests and the way the curtains opened on the transformation into flesh, the look on the congregants' faces as they took the mystery into their own very real bodies.

And all the time the new icons sitting on a table at the front, waiting to be blessed, and one of them was the one I'd struggled over.

Mother Catherine came back to sit by me when it was time for the blessing . She pointed out the other iconographers in the room. "Iconographer," she called me. The priest dropped holy water on my Mary's face and chanted a prayer, and Mother Catherine took me to the front of the line as everyone in the church stood to venerate the thing that I had made. I was, I knew, a fraud.

It's a tradition, Mother Catherine said, for the iconographer to be the first one to venerate the icon. How do I do that? I asked her. I was a fraud. *Like this,* she said, and I remembered that "like this" was one translation of the untranslatable word for God.

She showed me how to hold my hand and how to cross myself, head to navel, right shoulder to the left. And when I got to the icon, I made the sign, and it was one of the most unnatural things I've ever done.

But I was moved, and still am, by the way the congregants then made the sign and kissed the icon, and I realized that the Mary I'd struggled over for so long had sailed away, that she had her own life now beyond me, like my children, like this book, that for me she contained all the grief I'd felt for those who had passed or who would continue to pass through my life and my children's lives, for those who had died and for those who were yet to be born. That she would stay in my house above my desk, unvenerated probably as long as she stayed on my wall, a bit frightening at times, at times comforting. That through the years the light of the gold leaf behind her head will sometimes take me by surprise, that someday, maybe a hundred years from now, when I'm long gone, her light will shine as brightly as does the sunlight glazing the needles of the white pine tree outside my window on this particular sharp November day as I sit one last morning with this meditation, writing this one last line.

Susan Neville

is the author of five collections of creative
nonfiction and fiction, including *Invention of
Flight,* winner of the Flannery O'Connor
Award for Short Fiction; *In the House of Blue
Lights,* winner of the Richard Sullivan Fiction
Prize; and *Indiana Winter* (Indiana University
Press). Her stories and essays have appeared
in many magazines, including *The Georgia
Review, Northern American Review, The Crab
Orchard Review,* and *The Pushcart Prize*
anthology. She teaches creative writing at
Butler University in Indianapolis and is on
the faculty of the Warren Wilson MFA
Program for Writers.

Book and Cover Designer: Sharon L. Sklar

Copy Editor: Jane Lyle

Compositor: Sharon L. Sklar

Typeface: Berkeley

Book Printer: Thomson-Shore

Cover Printer: Pinnacle Press